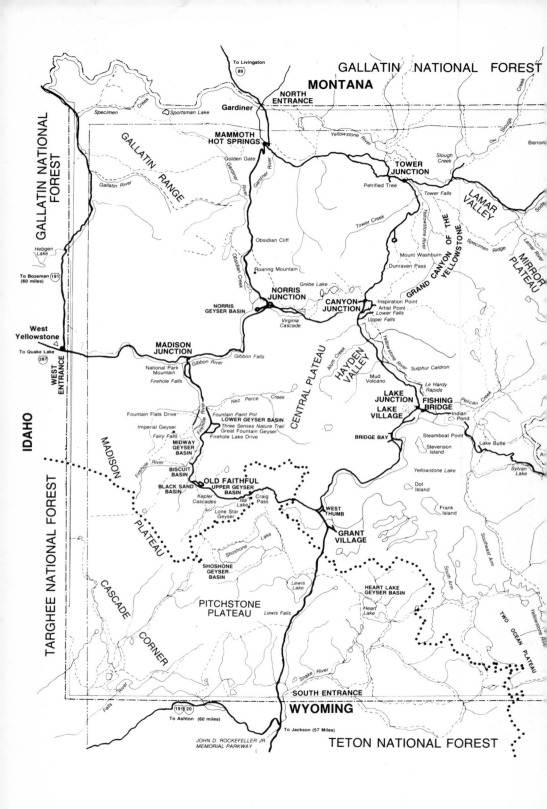

YELLOWSTONE
NATIONAL PARK

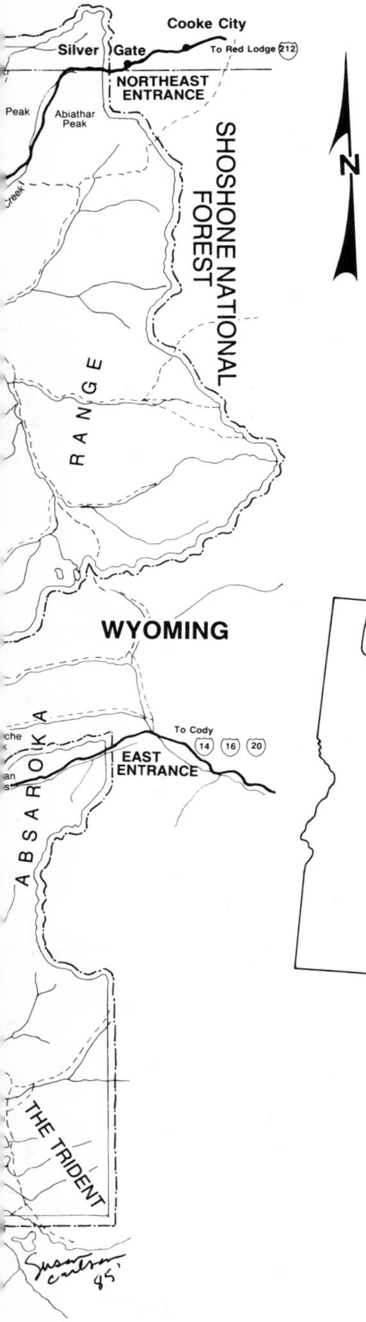

Cooke City
Silver Gate ● To Red Lodge (212)
**NORTHEAST
ENTRANCE**

Peak Abiathar
Peak

Creek

N

SHOSHONE NATIONAL
FOREST

RANGE

LEGEND
ROADS ————
TRAILS − − − − −
CONTINENTAL DIVIDE ● ● ● ● ● ●

Miles
0 1 2 3 4 5
0 1 2 3 4 5 6 7 8
Kilometers

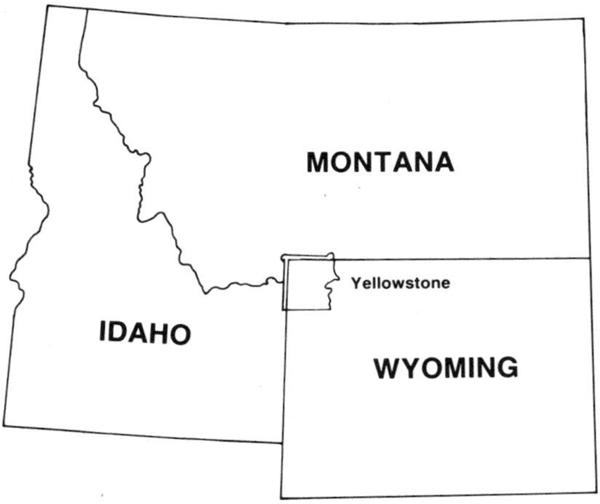

WYOMING

ABSAROKA

To Cody
(14) (16) (20)
che
**EAST
ENTRANCE**
an

MONTANA

Yellowstone

IDAHO

WYOMING

THE TRIDENT

Susan Carlson
85

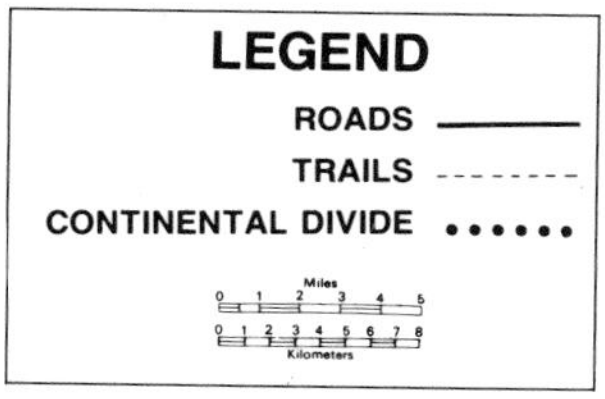

Young People's Guide To

YELLOWSTONE
NATIONAL PARK

By Robin Tawney

For Land & Mikal

Front cover photo by Mike Meloy
Back cover photo by Jan VanRiper
Copyright © 1985 Robin Tawney
All rights reserved
Published in the United States of America by Stoneydale
Press Publishing Co., Stevensville, Montana

Book Design by Susan Carlson

First Edition

Library of Congress Catalog Number 83-60358
ISBN 0-912299-04-5

PREFACE

When I first visited Yellowstone Park as a child, I did what a lot of other tourists did. I "saw" Yellowstone in a day, dashing to the park's most famous tourist attractions, like Old Faithful and the Grand Canyon of the Yellowstone. It wasn't until I was an adult that I really began to appreciate and get to know something of Yellowstone Park. Now I go back as often as I can, summer and winter. And I always take my own kids. Each time I visit the park, I learn something new.

I know how lucky I am to live in this part of the country where frequent Yellowstone visits are possible. Many people will be lucky if they see Yellowstone just once. With that in mind, I decided to write a book for young people that would help them get acquainted with their park and make them want to come back again.

Several people helped me along the way and they deserve my heartfelt thanks. Among them were Yellowstone Park Naturalists Norman Bishop, Jack DiGola and Joe Zarky; Chief Ranger Tom Hobbs; Rick and Mary Lee Reese, former directors of the Yellowstone Institute, and Bob Anderson, executive director of the Greater Yellowstone Coalition. Special thanks are due Ted Parkinson for the insight he imparted from his 37 seasons as a ranger-naturalist in Yellowstone and to North District Naturalist Tim Manns for his helpful review of my manuscript., to Mike Meloy and Dale Burk for allowing me to use photographs from their extensive files, and to my good friend Ellen Knight for spending so many long hours proofreading and indexing.

Special thanks also go to my husband Philip for his encouragement and patience, and to our children, Land and Mikal, ages 10 and 7 respectively, for sharing their wide-eyed enthusiasm as we explored Yellowstone Park together.

Robin Tawney
Missoula, Montana
May 1985

CONTENTS

WELCOME TO YELLOWSTONE NATIONAL PARK

A NATIONAL PARK IS BORN

FIRE AND ICE

THE GUIDE

THE GREATER YELLOWSTONE

Yellowstone Park is a land of geysers and hot springs, waterfalls, lakes and rivers, craggy peaks and open meadows. Come along and we will unlock its mysteries together. (Photo by Dale Burk)

WELCOME TO YELLOWSTONE NATIONAL PARK

Yellowstone National Park is the granddaddy of them all.

It is the world's oldest national park, established more than 100 years ago. It has more geysers and hot springs than the rest of the world combined. And it is big, covering 3,472 square miles — more than the states of Rhode Island and Delaware put together!

Yellowstone is indeed the "crown jewel" of America's national park system.

More than 2 million visitors come to Yellowstone each year, traveling from all parts of the United States and many foreign countries to see this vast park that straddles the backbone of the Northern Rocky Mountains, the Continental Divide. Tucked into the northwestern corner of Wyoming, most of the park lies within that state, but small portions ease over the state borders into Montana and Idaho as well.

If you've never been here before, you are in for a special treat. If this is your second, third or fourth trip, you are lucky. Each time you come to Yellowstone, you will learn something new about your park. Because really and truly knowing Yellowstone can take a lifetime.

This book is designed to help you get started. It is meant to be used. Go ahead, scribble notes and draw pictures in the margins. Blank pages in the back of the book have been reserved for your own Yellowstone journal or more extensive notes and drawings. This is one book that was meant to be soiled and dog-eared.

Before you begin your visit to Yellowstone Park, a couple of tips may be helpful: Yellowstone has only two real seasons, winter and summer. It can snow anytime of year and nights are always cool, even after the hottest days of summer, so be sure to bring warm clothes. Take that sweater or jacket plus raingear whenever you start out on a hike in Yellowstone. The weather can change very quickly and you will be more comfortable if you are well prepared!

Whatever the season, whatever you do here, try to keep in mind that everything you see affects everything else. The hot springs you will see, for example, are there because of the heat beneath the earth. Because they are where they are, the springs affect what kind of plants and animals live around them. How's that? Only certain plants can grow in or near the heavily mineralized hot springs deposits. And only certain animals can eat those plants.

Seeing and understanding how everything fits together is part of being human. Open your eyes, ears and noses to everything you come in contact with, and enjoy!

Snow in July? Anything's possible in Yellowstone. The weather can change quickly, so be prepared. (Photo by Mike Meloy)

Bighorn lambs grow up wild and free on the steep, rocky faces of Yellowstone's highest peaks. (Photo by Mike Meloy)

A National Park Is Not a Zoo

You won't see any giraffes or tigers roaming around Yellowstone National Park. No monkey houses or iron bars or fences either. What you will see, if you're lucky, are bison, moose, elk, deer, antelope and other animals who live here because this is their natural home. Oh, they may wander outside the park during some seasons, but they always come back. Instinct tells them this is their home.

How many animals you'll see while you are in Yellowstone will depend on the time of day, the time of year and the weather, among other things. In the summer, the best time of the day to see animals is in the very early morning or in the late evening. The largest animals bed down during the peak of the day and move around at night. In the winter, many of them are easier to see because they must spend their days in the open, foraging for food. All animals will seek shelter if it is rainy or stormy, so don't expect to see any then.

Wherever you go in the park, remember: Don't feed the animals and make sure you give all of them lots of room. Though many of the animals may look tame, they are all wild and potentially dangerous. Keep a safe distance. This is their home. You are the visitor.

Black bears used to beg treats from visitors. Now they live a healthier life in the backcountry. (Photo by Ed Wolff)

Bears

Maybe your parents have told you about how, when they visited Yellowstone as kids, the bears were everywhere. In fact, bold black bears would even stop cars along the highway to beg for food.

Those bears would create "bear jams" — backing up traffic as they milled around nibbling the scraps tourists would toss from their cars. Sometimes a bear would get a little over-eager when a tourist wasn't fast enough with the tidbits and it would climb right into the car.

Your parents may have watched grizzlies, too, as they fed on garbage thrown in open dumps around the park hotels. The hotels began this "tourist attraction" when people first started visiting Yellowstone in the late 1800s. Through all those years the grizzlies would come alone or with their families to eat whatever was thrown out. They put on quite a show.

Then in the late 1960s and early 1970s, the National Park Service, which administers Yellowstone, really cracked down. The service enforced the "no feeding" rule along the highways and closed the garbage dumps.

Now black bears, which actually range in color from black to blond, are scattered throughout the park. They are main-

Grizzlies need the wilderness that Yellowstone Park provides. (Photo by Montana's Department of Fish, Wildlife and Parks)

ly vegetarians, eating fruit, grass, insects and roots. But they will eat fresh meat, carrion (the bodies of dead animals), and fish, too.

Grizzly bears retreated to the wilderness sections of the park, for the most part. They are seldom seen along the highways or in developed areas. Since each bear requires solitude and hundreds of acres to roam, the grizzly is a good test of the quality of a wilderness. Yellowstone has that wilderness. The park is one of the few remaining homes for these great bears in the lower 48 states.

You can tell a grizzly from a black bear by its humped back, dished face and heavy body. Both bears eat the same things.

Both black bears and grizzlies also sleep all winter — they don't hibernate. Hibernating animals, like marmots, for example, have lowered body temperatures. Bears don't. If you were to stand outside a bear den, you would hear noises that mean that bear is just sleeping and that he might just wake up if you disturb him!

Although your chances of seeing a bear in Yellowstone aren't as good as they used to be, several thousand people do see bears each year. Keep an eye on open grassy areas like the Hayden Valley in early morning or late evening. You might just catch a bear looking for a meal.

Bison are plentiful in Yellowstone. Watch for them around watering holes, but don't try to approach them. Bison are wild and potentially dangerous. (Photo by Mike Meloy)

Bison

While you may not see a bear during your Yellowstone visit, you probably will see bison, moose, elk, mule deer, bighorn sheep and antelope. There are a lot more of these animals in the park and they tend to live in areas that are closer to the roads than the shy bears.

The mountain bison of Yellowstone are a sizable part of what is left of the millions that once roamed between the Atlantic Ocean and the Rocky Mountains. Today's bison live in the backcountry forests during the summer months, and spend their winters in the lower parts of the park, sometimes in the snow-free thermal basins and sometimes wading belly-deep in the snow.

If you visit the thermal areas in the summer, you will still see their huge footprints left from tramping in the soft mud and mineral deposits. You'll see their droppings, too, looking like huge brown frisbees.

Look for bull bison near watering holes. Cows and calves generally stay out of sight.

Watch for moose along the shorelines of lakes and streams where they feed on willows and aquatic plants. (Photo by Dale Burk)

Moose

Watch for moose, alone or in small groups, tramping the marshy meadows and shorelines of lakes and streams where they feed on willows and aquatic plants.

Like other members of the deer family, the bull moose sheds its antlers every year. (Cow moose don't grow them.) When you see a bull with its huge set of antlers, it is amazing to think that he sprouts those antlers in less than a year. Everything the bull needs to grow that magnificent rack and stay healthy is contained in the leaves and twigs the moose munches as he wades along.

Never underestimate the moose. A cow moose is especially dangerous if she has young ones to protect. While mother moose don't have antlers, they do have sharp hooves to kick.

During the winter, some elk move to lower areas outside the park. Others stay inside and are easily seen by winter visitors. (Photo by Mike Meloy)

Elk

Yellowstone has more elk than any other place in the world, so it shouldn't be surprising that elk outnumber all the other grazing animals here. The northern herd alone probably numbers around 16,000.

In summer, you can see elk in the high meadows throughout the park. There they graze on grasses, as well as browse like moose on shrubs, aspen bark and pine needles. In winter, some of the herds move to lower elevations outside the park, while others, numbering several thousand elk, remain inside. The elk that stay inside the park provide visitors with a real treat. Since the elk tend to stay at lower elevations and around the thermal areas, visitors can see the usually wary animals at close range.

Elk that are weakened by winter provide a major food source for predators and scavengers, especially grizzly bears when they leave their dens in the spring.

Mule Deer

Mule deer are named for their very large mule-like ears. During the summer these deer are scattered over most of the park in areas of broken forests and meadows. But since they can't survive the deep snow of winter, they drift down to lower, more open ranges, mostly outside the park.

Bighorn rams have large, curved horns. (Photo by Mike Meloy)

Bighorn Sheep

Bighorn sheep look like they may have come from a much earlier time, and they have. Many biologists believe that bighorns haven't changed much since the last glacier left the high country thousands of years ago.

Both males and females have horns. The males, or rams, have large, curved horns. The horns of the females, or ewes, are smaller and only slightly curved. Both have tan to gray coats with white rumps and stomachs.

During the summer, several hundred bighorn sheep live in the rugged mountain country of the park. Look for them there. Because their feet have spongy pads on the bottom, they can bounce from rock to rock without falling. In the winter, they move to lower elevations along the Yellowstone and Lamar rivers where they compete with elk and deer for winter range.

Chances are you won't see a pronghorn up close. They are shy creatures who prefer open areas where they watch for predators. (Photo by Ed Wolff)

Pronghorns

The pronghorn, or American antelope, is a plains animal with a body just made for speed and agility. Pronghorns depend upon their keen eyesight to protect them from predators. They prefer open, rather than forested, areas. Through the winter they stay in the lowest part of the park north of Mammoth Hot Springs, where the snow is least deep. In the spring, some pronghorns will migrate up the Yellowstone River to the Lamar Valley, grazing away the summer there.

Watch for their tan bodies with distinctive white stripes across their throats and white bellies and rumps. Both male and female have hollow branched horns and each year shed the outer sheath or layer.

Other Animals

While you are enjoying Yellowstone's largest animals, don't forget to look for the small ones around you as well. The park is rich with an abundance of critters — from the tiniest brine flies hovering over the hot springs to the scarce mountain lion stalking its prey.

Many of the mammals scamper about in the daytime, but others are active only at night. Several kinds of mice, woodrats and flying squirrels go about their business under the cover of darkness, but others, like chipmunks (with stripes on their sides and faces) and golden-mantled ground squirrels (larger than chipmunks with stripes just on their sides) can be seen any time of day.

Keep an eye out for nature's plows in open, grassy areas of the park. See if you can tell if the freshly tilled soil you find is the work of ants, pocket gophers or bears. Anthills will be neat round mounds. Pocket gophers leave lopsided mounds as they cover up the openings to their tunnels. Bears are anything but neat as they chase after their fellow "plows." They leave tumbles of soil as they dig for food stored by the pocket gophers and the gophers themselves! Sometime you might come upon a meadow that looks totally topsy-turvy. It is likely a bear was at work there.

You will see golden-mantled ground squirrels just about everywhere in the park. These perky animals have stripes down their backs, but not on their faces. (Photo by Robin Tawney)

By being very still, you can watch one mammal make a magical transformation from a rockchuck to a groundhog to a woodchuck to a whistlepig — just by moving from a rock to his burrow in the ground to the woods where he gives a shrill, whistle-like call. That is because rockchuck, groundhog, woodchuck and whistlepig all are names for the yellowbelly marmot!

Look for coyotes in the open meadows of the park, stalking ground squirrels and mice. Or you might see them around the hot springs where they watch for birds that are warming themselves or snacking on insects in the runoff channels. Sometimes those birds are suffocated by gases coming from the springs. When that happens, some people think that coyotes, unbothered by the gases, snatch up the birds. No one has ever really seen the coyotes raid the hot springs. Maybe you will be the first.

If you are a good observer, you may have the chance to see many other mammals (not to mention birds, fish and insects!) while you are in the park. Many of them will be described in detail in portions of this book covering those areas they are most likely to haunt.

But even though you may not see a great variety of animals, it is nice just to know they are there. Remember, you are a visitor in their home and you are always being watched — by someone or something.

Trees, Trees and More Trees

You'll see more trees than animals as you tour the park, that's for sure! Among those trees, you might notice that three different types of evergreens stand out. And while you will see all three in most parts of the park, you'll usually see more of one kind of these trees in one particular area because it grows better there.

For example, the Douglas fir is found between Mammoth

Hot Springs and the Lamar Valley. Lodgepole pines grow mostly in the central portion of the park and in scattered areas to the south. The rest of Yellowstone is covered with Englemann spruce and Douglas fir, mixed with lodgepole.

How do you tell these trees apart? It is fairly simple if you have a few clues.

Most of the lodgepoles you see will be in "toothpick forests" where they grow so tightly packed together, their lower branches die and drop off because they don't get enough sun to grow. If a lodgepole grows all by itself, it will look just like a Christmas tree with full branches all the way to the ground.

But no matter where they grow in Yellowstone, all lodgepole pines have straight and even trunks. They got their name because American Indians used them as poles for tepees and lodges. Which lodgepole would you choose for your tepee: One growing in a thick stand with few branches, or one growing all alone with many branches? Which would be easiest to use?

When a lodgepole dies, it leaves a hole in the sky for another tree to grow. But even though the lodgepoles drop their cones like other trees, you often won't find any young lodgepoles on the forest floor. Many lodgepole pine cones do not open unless a forest fire heats them up. Then one or two days after the fire, the seeds from the cones will be released in a shower. They will grow readily in the raw earth of the scorched forest floor. Because lodgepoles are among the first plants to grow after a fire, they are called pioneers.

On the other hand, Engelmann spruce and Douglas fir forests are climax forests. That means these trees dominate the areas where they are found, although other kinds of trees grow there, too. These forests will not change unless they are cleared by wind, flood, fire or other catastrophe. Natural disasters do take place, however, and allow the lodgepole pine to germinate and thrive and remain the most common tree in the park.

The Engelmann spruce is shaped like a pyramid, with drooping cones and branches that have short needles all along them. The Douglas fir looks similar, but its cones stand

Engelmann Spruce

Douglas Fir

Lodgepole Pine

Lodgepole Pine Forest

upright on its limbs. To be sure which is which, you just have to remember some simple facts:

The spruce has sharp, square (if you looked at one from the end), stiff needles attached to the branch singly. The fir has flat, flexible and friendly (no prickles) needles attached to the branch by twos. Get the point?

When you look up at the trees of Yellowstone, sometimes you'll see strange, deforming growths in a cluster of branches. Mistletoe does that — the same stuff we hang at Christmas to steal a kiss!

Other trees grow beards. That blackish-green moss you see hanging down is called Old Man's Beard.

If you put a little bit in your mouth for a couple of minutes, it will turn green from the moisture.

All green plants give us oxygen to breathe. When we ex-
hale, or let out our breath, carbon dioxide comes out. The
trees and other plants need carbon dioxide to grow and stay
healthy. So breathe deeply in Yellowstone Park — and give
the trees a picnic!

Be a Wilderness Detective

As you walk through the woods, look for fur stuck on the
trunks and branches of the trees. That means that some
animal has been using that tree for a back-scratching post to
rub off its itchy winter coat. See if you can tell what kind of
animal stopped to scratch.

Look for clues of things that don't fit. You just might come
across evidence of early park visitors. They weren't very
careful with their garbage, so you might find pieces of bot-
tles, plates and tins, even building foundations and water
valves from old water systems. Remember to leave
whatever you find where you find it so others can enjoy their
own discovery.

Look for animal droppings or scat along game trails. Ask a
ranger to help you identify your finds.

Take along a magnifying glass and a glass jar. Scoop up
some water from a stream or lake and watch the creatures
you have caught. Release them back into the water.

Get down on your knees and take a nature creep for a
couple of yards and you will see lots of plants, insects and
animal tracks you wouldn't see otherwise. We often
overlook this mini-world because we are four or five feet
above it.

The more you learn about the natural world, the more
you'll understand.

Now let's begin our exploration of the natural wonders of
Yellowstone by learning something about the history of our
first national park!

Members of the 1871 Hayden expedition eat lunch at their camp at Red Buttes. (National Park Service Photo)

A NATIONAL PARK IS BORN

To hear the mountain men tell it, the Yellowstone area sounded like an enchanted land.

One of those men, Jim Bridger, told tall tales of glass mountains and of forests where everything had turned to stone. He said you could see right through those mountains of glass. And that petrified birds perched on petrified trees sang petrified songs in which every note turned to stone!

But the mountain men weren't the only people who thought there was something special about this place. Native Americans had felt that way for a long time, but most of them were afraid to stay too long in this land of bubbling hot springs and wild, unpredictable geysers. Only the Sheepeater Indians lived in what is now Yellowstone National Park. They had to stay close to home because they didn't have horses like the other tribes. Still they managed to kill plenty of bighorn sheep, using the meat and hides for their food and clothing. That is how they got their name.

The tall tales spun by trappers who came here long before Jim Bridger to trade with the Sheepeaters eventually reached people who lived in more civilized surroundings. While the far-fetched stories were almost beyond belief, people began to guess that there was something incredibly wonderful about this country.

Yet despite these tales about the curiosities of Yellowstone, the most famous explorers of the early 1800s passed them up. The Lewis and Clark Expedition of

1804-06 was sent out west by President Thomas Jefferson to explore the new frontier and to find out how it could benefit the new United States of America. They were looking for furs and trade routes, not for geysers and hot springs.

While Lewis and Clark did not explore Yellowstone, one of the men who travelled with them did after he left the Expedition. That man was John Colter. He was hired by one of the first fur trading posts along the Yellowstone River to find Indian customers. He saw the geysers of Yellowstone and told stories about his adventures.

Colter's news about the geysers and about all the animals he found in the Rocky Mountains brought many other explorers and fur trappers into the area. Hats made out of beaver pelts were in style, and this country was loaded with beaver.

Mountain men like Jim Bridger, Jedediah Smith and Daniel Potts headed for Yellowstone, searching for furs. They all saw the fantastic things John Colter had spoken of and began to tell stories of their own. Since storytelling was the main form of entertainment for these wild and wooly men, the stories they told were, more often than not, exaggerated to "top" the last stories they had heard.

Their tall tales reached other trappers and fur traders who came to Yellowstone to see for themselves what they called "Colter's Hell" and the "unlimited" fur supply.

The Word Spreads

As more trappers came West, they trapped more and more beavers, and the beavers began to disappear. Around 1840 the lack of beaver pelts for fine fur hats and a change in fashion (to black silk hats) ended the fur trade.

The discovery of gold in Montana brought explorers back to the upper Yellowstone in 1863. This time they searched for a bit of "color" that might indicate a large body of gold ore. No metals of real value were found within the park boundaries, but the would-be miners sparked new interest in Yellowstone.

Three major exploring parties visited the area in 1869,

The Hayden Survey party launched the first boat ever on Yellowstone Lake in 1871. (National Park Service Photo)

1870 and 1871. The first of these was to be led by Montana Territory's Acting Governor Thomas F. Meagher in 1865. Meagher felt that if the area was as wonderful as reports had it, it deserved to be set aside as a national park — preserved for all people for all time. Unfortunately, Meagher died the night before his party was to leave, and the expedition was postponed.

Other men began to think like Meagher and wanted Yellowstone to be set aside as a national park. One of these men was David E. Folsom, who led the expedition Meagher had planned, in 1869. Another was Cornelius Hedges, who participated in the 1870 expedition.

At the same time, Northern Pacific Railroad Co. was anxious to use the wonders of Yellowstone to attract customers for the railroad service it was building to the West Coast. In fact, in 1871 an agent for the Northern Pacific suggested: "Let Congress pass a bill reserving the Great Geyser Basin as a public park forever . . .."

And Congress did. Unlike practically any proposal before Congress today, the bill establishing Yellowstone National Park was passed with little debate. President Ulysses S. Grant signed the bill into law on March 1, 1872.

The Northern Pacific Railroad became the principal means of access to Yellowstone and its first concessioner, providing lodging and food for tourists just like the concessioner does today.

Yellowstone Becomes a National Park

The bill making Yellowstone a national park passed at a time when other federal laws promised every American family its share of the new frontier. At that point in history, most people were more interested in what they could get out of the land than in preserving it.

Millions of acres were being reserved for use by the railroads. Lumbermen were cutting acres and acres and acres of timber without even thinking about replanting trees to provide lumber in the future. Cattlemen were grazing vast herds of cattle that ate every blade of grass and left bare ground wherever they went. Hunters were urged to kill bison by the thousands so that the Plains Indians, who depended on the shaggy beasts for their food and clothing, could be easily controlled.

With these kinds of attitudes about using up natural resources like land, trees, grass and bison, it is no wonder that early Yellowstone tourists felt the same way about the

Army rangers bring in a poacher who was killing bison inside park boundaries. The year: 1894. (National Park Service Photo)

geyser formations of Yellowstone. They used shovels and axes to chop and hack and pry up great pieces of the geysers. They threw objects into the geysers to see how far the debris would shoot up when they erupted.

The act that established Yellowstone National Park provided no special laws or money for government regulation. There was no money to build roads or to protect the park from vandalism. There wasn't even any money to pay the park's first superintendent, Nathaniel P. Langford.

As more people came to the park each year, pieces of geyser formations were broken off and hauled away. Rich sportsmen and hunters slaughtered the elk and deer, often taking only their trophy antlers, hides, and, in the case of elk, their ivory teeth.

U.S. Cavalry to the Rescue

At last, after years of abuse, it was obvious that something had to be done. Congress sent the U.S. Cavalry to restore order to the park on Aug. 20, 1886.

The Army collected scientific information and built road and trail systems that are still in use today. They built many of the buildings at park headquarters at Mammoth Hot Springs.

The Army also patrolled the park to stop the poachers and vandals because the soldiers had begun to see that it was important to preserve all that was natural within the park, not just the geothermal features. One of the results of this policy was the preservation and restoration of the American bison, an animal that was almost wiped out in the 1890s. You can read about what the Army did to save the bison in the guide section on Lamar Ranger Station.

Because of the Army's efforts to preserve all the wildlife, nearly all our national parks today, including Yellowstone, are wildlife refuges. (Hunting is permitted under some circumstances in some of Alaska's national parks.)

Early visitors toured the park by stagecoach, carriage and horseback. (National Park Service Photo)

The ranger-naturalist program we know today began when the soldiers at Yellowstone were told to explain the natural curiosities to visitors when they were asked. In 1908 the acting superintendent asked the government for books on natural history for the "better education and information" of the protectors of the park. When the National Park Service was established in 1916, it was staffed by these trained men. Today you will see rangers and naturalists in their green and gray uniforms everywhere you go in the park. Just like the rangers of yesterday, these people are trained to answer your questions.

This 1903 photograph shows park headquarters at Fort Yellowstone, or Mammoth Hot Springs as we now know it. (National Park Service Photo)

National Park Service Rangers Dunrud and Douglas patrolled Yellowstone on skis in 1927. (National Park Service Photo)

The magma that keeps Yellowstone's hot pots and geysers sizzling is just two to five miles beneath the ground's surface. Take note of what you see. These hot water features are constantly changing. (Photo by Robin Tawney)

FIRE AND ICE

Remember when the volcano Mt. St. Helens blew its top in 1980? Remember how the ash from that explosion spread across the western states?

Now imagine a volcano that exploded with 2,500 (that's 25 one hundreds!) times the force of Mt. St. Helens. Sulfuric ash from the Yellowstone blast fell all over the world. That volcanic eruption of 600,000 years ago and two other more recent ones helped form the area we know as Yellowstone National Park.

But volcanoes are just one part of the geology of the park. Earthquakes, seas and glaciers all have played a role in forming the landscape. Knowing about these things and how the fire deep in the earth still affects Yellowstone will help you better understand what you see as you explore the park.

How Do Mountains Begin?

The mountain ranges north, south and east of the central part of the park were formed by an intense period of mountain building and volcanic eruptions 2.7 **billion** years ago — long before there were people or trees, or even dinosaurs. It is hard to imagine how long ago that was, so let's look at it this way: If you stepped back in time, and one step equaled 100 years, one step would take you to 1875, three years after Yellowstone National Park was established.

Now if you wanted to reach the period when the park's geologic features were first forming, you would have to walk across the United States five times or about half-way around the world — a total distance of about 15,000 miles!

Two billion seven hundred million years ago, the earth was hot and fiery, much too hot for anything to live on it. And even when the earth finally cooled on the outside, it stayed boiling hot on the inside.

Here and there, some of the magma, the mixture of gas and hot melted rock deep inside the earth, squeezed through cracks and holes on the earth's surface. Or sometimes the magma was pushed out in a big blast — a volcanic eruption.

However the magma came out, it cooled and hardened after it came out of the ground. More hot melted rock poured out on top of the newly hardened rock, and then it cooled and became hard, too. Sometimes this happened over and over until a big pile of cooled lava had grown to be a mountain.

Some of the mountains in Yellowstone Park were formed by pressures within the earth that pushed at the earth's surface from all sides. These earthquakes were so strong that, for miles and miles, the rock on top would break and turn on edge. Part of the earth would then be lower and part of it higher.

You can see how this happened if you put your hands on two sides of some wet sand or mud, and then push your hands together slowly. The sand or mud will rise between your hands and become all wrinkled and folded — the way many of the mountains look in Yellowstone National Park.

The Inland Ocean

After the first period of mountain building, the area was flooded from time to time by seas that stretched from Canada to Mexico. Water would cover all but the highest mountain peaks for a long while, then it would dry up. Another flood would follow and then that water would dry up, too. So it went for many, many years.

Each time the area flooded, another sea bed of sand, silt, clay, limy mud and other sediments would settle in the bottom of the sea. This loose material would harden into rock when the water was gone. You can see evidence of the many sea beds in the "layered cake" effect of these sandstones, shales and limestone. Fossils of some hard-shelled animals that lived in the long-ago seas can be found in some of these rocks.

Often the ancient sea beds were severely twisted and broken by later mountain-building movements. Just think how powerful the force must have been to twist and break the earth like that!

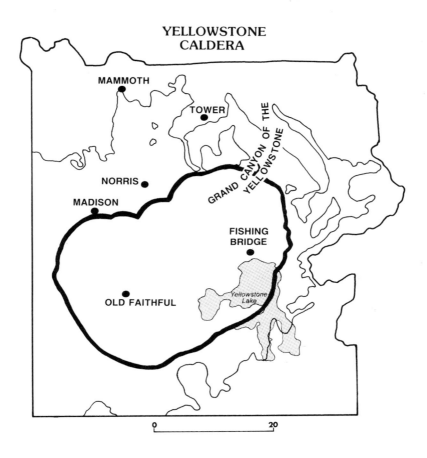

YELLOWSTONE
CALDERA

MAMMOTH

TOWER

GRAND CANYON OF THE YELLOWSTONE

NORRIS

MADISON

FISHING
BRIDGE

OLD FAITHFUL

Yellowstone
Lake

0   20

Fire in the Earth

After the last sea disappeared, forces within the earth began new rumblings. At last a series of new volcanoes erupted that gave the park many of the major features we see today. The biggest blast happened 600,000 years ago, or less than half a mile if you step back in time. (Remember, one step equals 100 years!)

That blast was greater than any volcanic eruption in recorded history. Far greater than Mt. St. Helens and a far bigger blast than even Krakatoa. Krakatoa, a volcano on the island of Java in the South Seas, erupted in 1883 with a roar that was heard 3,000 miles away in Australia!

The big blast in Yellowstone was really a series of rapid, violent explosions as hundreds of cubic miles of hot rock and ash poured from two magma chambers. All this material spread quickly over the central portion of Yellowstone, filling canyons and valleys that had eroded, or worn away, some of the lava flows of earlier explosions.

Some of the liquid rock hardened and formed a new roof over the magma chambers. Since tons and tons of rock had been blown from underground, there was nothing to support this new ground surface and huge chunks of rock fell in above each of the chambers.

After the big blast in Yellowstone, the lava that poured out cooled and made a hard pile over the gaping mouth of the volcano. More and more lava poured out, and the pile eventually became a dome — like an upside down bowl — with the still fiery magma beneath. Without anything solid to support it from below, the dome finally collapsed and formed a gigantic crater, or caldera, 30 miles across, 45 miles long and about a mile deep.

Like toothpaste, lava began oozing from cracks in the new surface. As the still smouldering caldera filled up, it became the low rolling plateau that includes a third of the park's area. Yellowstone Lake fills the southeastern portion of the caldera.

Rivers of Ice

During the quiet times between volcanic eruptions, all but the highest mountain peaks and the western edge of the park were again flooded, but this time, not by water — by ice. At least three glaciers covered the area.

Glaciers are formed when more snow accumulates during winter than can melt in summer. If this continues for hundreds of years, the snow gets so deep and heavy that the snow on the bottom is crushed into ice by the weight of the snow on top. This is like when you pack a snowball between your hands. As you squeeze the snow, it becomes almost like ice instead of soft, loose snow. That is just what happens when a glacier is formed.

These rolling hills along the Yellowstone River are really rubble that was pushed along by a glacier long ago. (Photo by Dale Burk)

Each winter the icefields grow, and each summer some of the snow on top is melted by the sun. The melted snow water sinks down, mixing with the bottom snow, and freezes. This packing and pressing and freezing keeps on until the whole ice field finally begins to move because of its sheer weight.

When the ice begins to move it becomes a glacier, a river of solid ice moving between the mountains. But instead of moving swiftly like a regular river, the glacier moves so slowly it looks like it is standing still.

As the glacier moves, no more than a few feet each day, it scrapes the sides of the mountains and tears off chunks of rocks, sometimes as big as houses. Big rocks, little rocks, sand and clay all are scooped up by the moving ice and carried along.

At last the glacier moves down the mountains into warmer weather, and the ice begins to melt. As it melts, large boulders and sand are dropped and the water rushes into streams. The boulders — glacial erratics — are stranded wherever they drop from the melting glacier.

You'll find these almost black glacial erratics scattered all over the park. Notice their smooth and rounded edges. The sharp points on these rocks were ground down as they were scooted along with the rocks, sand and other materials in the glacier, just like pebbles are smoothed as they roll along the bottom of a stream.

Some of the rock debris left by the Yellowstone glaciers as they melted formed natural dams across stream valleys, which created lakes. Then some of these glacial dams broke and caused giant floods, pushing more rocks and debris in front of them.

The scraping, grinding and gouging of the glaciers also rounded hills and scooped out basins, called cirques, high in the mountains. You can see these bowl-shaped depressions in some of the mountains as you drive through the park.

Today, even though a few snowfields last all summer, no glaciers exist in Yellowstone Park. But if the temperatures dropped just a few degrees or the yearly snowfall increased a foot or so, either change could mean the beginning of a new ice age in Yellowstone.

Look Inside the Earth's Interior

You can watch geology happening right before your eyes every day of the year when you visit the geothermal features that made Yellowstone famous. (You will see both geothermal and hydrothermal used to describe Yellowstone's hot water features. "Geo" means earth, "hydro" means water, and "thermal" means heat. So "geothermal" means heat from the earth's interior and "hydrothermal" means hot water, especially the water heated from the magma deep in the ground. You can use either term to describe Yellowstone's hot water features.)

Yellowstone has 10,000 geothermal features scattered throughout the park. Most of these features are clustered in a few areas called geyser basins. The geysers and hot springs are here because magma from the most recent volcanoes is still very hot just three to five miles beneath the surface of the basins. In some areas, the magma is boiling hot less than two miles below. These underground temperatures haven't cooled off since the park began to keep records more than 100 years ago!

Water to feed the hot springs is abundant because each winter as much as 200 inches of snow falls on the park, settling into a five-foot blanket. When summer comes, this snow melts and water flows into the rivers and lakes and seeps into the huge natural reservoirs underground. There it is heated by the hot rocks deep in the earth and forced back to the surface, creating hot springs, fumaroles and geysers.

Hot Springs, Fumaroles and Geysers

Now it is time to learn about some of the special features that make Yellowstone National Park famous.

Hot springs form as heated water rises to the surface of the ground through a series of tubes, much like the pipes that deliver water to your sink. Sometimes the water collects in pools and sometimes it spills over to form terraces like those at Mammoth Hot Springs. Some hot springs are so hot they are boiling!

HOW A HOT SPRING WORKS

Water from snow and rain seeps into the ground. Magma heats rock far below the ground surface and sends hot gases upwards. The water is heated by these rocks and gases and is forced back to the surface. It is now bubbling and steaming.

Steam vents or fumaroles are hot springs, but their water supplies are so limited, the heat below turns water into steam immediately. Steam rises through the fumaroles' plumbing with a hiss or a roar.

When water collects around fumaroles, it mixes with clay and undissolved minerals and forms **mud pots**. As steam rises, it bubbles through the clay, making a "soup." Mud pots are most active in winter through early summer when rain and snow help moisten the mud.

Geysers are hot springs with complicated plumbing systems. In fact no two geysers have the same size, shape and arrangements of tubes and chambers through which water passes to and from the surface.

We can't see the actual plumbing of any geyser, but we

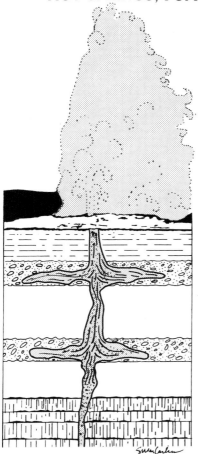

HOW A GEYSER WORKS

No one can know what a geyser's plumbing really looks like because it is far below the ground. Scientists guess, however, that geysers work something like this: After an eruption, the tubes and chambers of a geyser refill with water that has been stored in chambers, side channels or layers of porous rock. As that water is heated by the thermal source below, some of it turns into steam bubbles. Those bubbles multiply in number and size as they rise to the surface. They get caught in tight passageways and push water and steam to the surface and the geyser erupts. When most of the extra energy is spent and the geyser tubes and chambers are nearly empty, the eruption ends. The system again begins to fill with water and the cycle starts over.

can guess how it works. Scientists tell us that superheated water and gas rise in the tubes and get stuck momentarily. This makes pressure build up in the water and gas below. The pressure gets so great, the "dam" is burst and the water and gas surge to the ground's surface and the geyser erupts. When the geyser tubes and chambers are nearly empty, the eruption ends and the process of refilling with groundwater begins again.

Yellowstone has more geysers than the rest of the world combined. At least 60 of its 200 geysers shoot water to heights of 10 feet or more.

Each geyser follows its own particular pattern and might not have regular eruptions. Some spout nearly all the time, others seem to be on cycles with eruptions that are days, months and even years apart.

Hot Springs Deposits

Nearly all geysers and many hot springs build mounds or terraces made up of many very thin layers of mineral deposits. Built up over hundreds of years, each layer represents a crust or film of rock-forming mineral that was originally dissolved in hot water, as salt is dissolved when you add it to hot water. Although you can't see the salt any more, you know it is there because you can taste it. That means the salt dissolved in the water. (Don't taste the hot springs water. It could make you sick.) The rotten egg smell some people associate with hot springs comes from dissolved sulfur, which, when mixed with water, forms hydrogen sulfide gas.

The water in a geyser or hot spring picks up minerals as it flows through underground rocks. When pressures build, the water rises and spreads out over the surrounding ground, and then dries up, leaving the rock-forming mineral behind. The new surface is white or gray in color.

Terraces of the new rock that are constantly underwater may be brightly colored because they are covered with tiny, tiny plants called algae. The algae may be green, yellow or brown and may make a hot spring pool appear that color. Other colors occur because of minerals coating the walls and bottom of the spring or suspended in the water. Some pools are too hot to allow algae to grow. Those pools are usually blue, reflecting the blue sky overhead off their sides and bottoms.

You will notice white socks on trees around the hot springs. These trees were growing there before the hot springs formed or spread. As they became surrounded by the springs, they were gradually choked by the heat and mineral deposits. Minerals, which give the trees their white socks, gradually replaced the material in the tree trunks. The trees became petrified.

Take careful note of what you see and write it down in the margins or on the blank pages in the back of this book. You will surprised at how the thermal features have changed by the time you visit Yellowstone again. Sometimes formations

The Hebgen Lake Earthquake site still looks raw 25 years later. (Photo by Dale Burk)

will change a lot between the time you enter and leave the park.

Earthquakes

Another kind of geologic change is occurring daily in Yellowstone National Park, although chances are you won't be able to tell. Sensitive instruments called seismographs record an average of five earth tremors daily in and around the park. This is normal for an area with such a violent history of volcanic activity and previous earthquakes.

Once in a very long while, seismographs may even record over 100 tremors a day. Most of these quakes are so slight, you wouldn't feel them, but once in a human lifetime, a big one hits.

This huge landslide dammed the Madison River and formed Earthquake Lake. (Photo by Dale Burk)

The biggest recorded earthquake to affect Yellowstone hit on Aug. 17, 1959. The Hebgen Lake Earthquake was centered in the Madison Valley along the western boundary of the park about 12 miles north of West Yellowstone. Much of the earth in a 200 square mile area, including Hebgen Lake, sank from 1 to 20 feet. The quake also caused noticeable water level changes in water wells as far away as Puerto Rico to the east and Hawaii to the west.

A huge landslide trapped 250 campers and killed 28 of them. The slide dammed the Madison River and formed Earthquake Lake. Inside Yellowstone Park, nearly 300 geysers and hot springs erupted soon after the earthquake hit. One hundred sixty of these had never before erupted. Some geysers that had been "dead" for a long time erupted immediately after the quake. Others erupted with much greater force or frequency. Still others stopped erupting entirely and have not spouted since.

If you leave or enter the park through Yellowstone's West Entrance, stop at the Forest Service visitor center at the top of the slide that formed Earthquake Lake. It is open only during the summer.

What Does the Future Hold?

Yellowstone will always be an unsettled place. Its long history of volcanic activity and earthquakes means that someday — maybe not in your lifetime — things will fly sky-high once again. As you explore the park, you will be constantly reminded of how quickly formations change. The hot water and steam that come from deep in the earth will build up and tear down formations as you watch

Scientists say that any new volcanic activity probably will be preceded by localized earthquakes and increased gas emissions. They say future earthquakes will certainly take place and may be at least as strong or stronger than the Hebgen Lake Earthquake. But don't worry, Yellowstone Park is monitored by all sorts of fancy scientific equipment. You should get plenty of warning if something big is about to happen!

Taking a nature walk with a park ranger is one of the best ways to learn about Yellowstone. Here a ranger helps visitors unlock the secrets of a lodgepole pine forest near Yellowstone Lake. (Photo by Robin Tawney)

THE GUIDE

Now that you know something about the history and geology of Yellowstone, it is time to explore the park.

Stop to hike the trails as often as you can. You can't get to know the park through the windows of your car, bus or camper. You have to get out and smell the pines, the sulfur and the wet earth. Feel the heat from the steaming hot springs and the wind-blown spray from the geysers as you walk along the paths and boardwalks of the thermal areas. Hear the caw-caw of ravens, the thunderous roar of water as it falls over the brink of a waterfall, the splattering and gurgling of the mud pots, the chatter of golden-mantled ground squirrels as they beg.

In nature, every smell, touch and sound has a meaning. Pay attention to them all.

Try to take in the nightly ranger talks in the amphitheaters of the various settlements around the park. They will help you understand what you are learning about Yellowstone. Pick up maps and information from visitor centers everywhere you go. And try to join a ranger-naturalist for a special walk or daytime program. Both are offered free of charge summer and winter.

Be a Smart Park Visitor

Remember you are in a wild place, where everything is in as natural a state as possible. This means there are special hazards. Among them:

• Thermal areas. As you enjoy the hot springs and geysers of Yellowstone, stay on the boardwalks and trails. Each year tourists are injured when they get too near the boiling water and fall through the thin crusts around the

Stay on the boardwalks! They are there to keep you safe. (Photo by Robin Tawney)

pools. Whoever said "better safe than sorry" was right! (People can get hurt when they try to rescue their pets, too. That's why the park says NO PETS on the boardwalk and trails of the thermal basins.)

• Bears. Food attracts bears to campgrounds, so make sure your food is properly stowed away. Lock it up in your car or hang it 10 feet above the ground and 5 feet out from a post or tree. Keep your camp clean so you won't have a night visitor!

• Other animals. Although the animals you see appear calm and well adjusted to visitors pointing cameras at them, every one of them is wild and potentially dangerous. That bull elk calmly "posing" for a picture could charge you in an instant. Bears and moose are especially aggressive. And that tiny ground squirrel who would like to share your lunch might just share a disease with you, too. Watch all animals from a safe distance, or better yet, from your car. Don't feed any of them.

• Backcountry travel. While visiting the backcountry by foot, horseback or boat is a special way to get to know Yellowstone, it also presents special hazards. Encounters with bears and other large animals are more frequent in the backcountry. Cold, deep water and the possibility of sudden storms are special problems for boaters and anglers to consider. See a ranger for a permit before you enter the backcountry or fish. Permits for both are required by law.

If you obey all these rules, walking across the highway could be the most dangerous thing you do while you're in Yellowstone National Park!

How to Use the Guide

Speaking of highways, Yellowstone has over 300 miles of paved roads. Nearly half that distance is covered by the Grand Loop, a rough figure 8 that passes near the park's most famous features.

To begin your journey, look for the name of the place where you enter Yellowstone in the Table of Contents at the front of this book. Then follow along section by section as you visit each area of the park. Where appropriate, short notes explain what type of facilities you'll find at the major crossroads and points of interest.

Now, come along with me and let's explore Yellowstone together!

West Entrance to Madison Junction

If you enter the park right outside West Yellowstone, Montana, you'll travel down the broad, flat **Madison River Valley**. A couple of miles from the park entrance, the road begins to run alongside the **Madison River**, rushing back toward Montana. You'll soon leave Montana and enter Wyoming.

The river you are following was named by the Lewis and Clark Expedition in 1805 for James Madison, who was then secretary of state under President Thomas Jefferson and later the fourth president of the United States. While Lewis and Clark never saw this portion of the Madison, or any of the territory that would become Yellowstone National Park, they became acquainted with the section of the river in southcentral Montana where it joins with the Gallatin and the Jefferson rivers to form the mighty Missouri.

Try to imagine what this country would look like without the cars, roads and other signs of civilization. Now imagine you are an early trapper. This is the same route the trappers took as they followed the Madison River upstream to its headwaters — the place where the Gibbon and Firehole rivers join to form the Madison. Later, when roads were first built into the park, stagecoaches and carriages also rumbled along this route.

How do you think those big boulders ended up in the river? Look up at the hills above the Madison and see if you can tell. The 1959 earthquake caused rockslides, sending tons of rocks crashing and mashing whatever was in their path. Many of those rocks landed in the river.

The Madison is one of the best trout streams in America. Make sure you ask a ranger for a free fishing permit and a copy of Yellowstone Park fishing regulations. Then stop at one of the many fishing access sites along the river and try your luck. You will find brown and rainbow trout and whitefish, too. Happy fishing!

Watch for Canada geese, great blue herons and ducks along the river. Keep a sharp eye out for the graceful white trumpeter swans near the bridge that crosses the Madison. With wingspans of 8 feet, these birds are the largest swans in the United States. Years ago, they almost became extinct. Let's learn something more about them:

Watch for trumpeter swans along the Madison River. You'll know these white birds by their long, graceful necks and 8-foot wingspans. (Photo by Jack Tuholske)

Trumpeters once nested and fed by the thousands from the Arctic to the Gulf Coast, and from the Pacific to the marshes of Indiana and northern Missouri. Then they became prized for their feathers and soft down. Feathers were made into decorations and writing quills and the down was used for powder puffs.

During the early 1800s fur companies handled as many as 2,000 swanskins in a year. Most of the skins were sold in England, although American colonists hunted and used swans, too. Despite the vast numbers of swans, they were hunted too much, and the species came close to vanishing.

By 1932 only 69 trumpeters existed in the U.S., not counting Alaska. These swans were discovered by a park biologist at **Red Rocks Lake**, Montana, just west of Yellowstone Park. Three years later Red Rocks was set aside as a national wildlife refuge. There the trumpeters were fed grain and carefully protected. And slowly their flocks began to rebuild.

Today between 4,000 and 5,000 trumpeter swans nest in Yellowstone and a few other places in the West. Look for them along the Madison River and in Hayden Valley along the Yellowstone River.

When you come to the headwaters of the Madison — about where the West Entrance Road meets the Grand Loop — stop for a moment and look across the river. In 1870 the 19 members of the Washburn-Langford-Doane Expedition spent their last night in Yellowstone on the point of land between the two rivers. Around the campfire that night, the men talked about what should be done with the area. Some men said they thought claims should be staked on the most scenic regions. In later years, some participants said that others borrowed an older idea and suggested that the entire area be set aside as a national park for the benefit and enjoyment of all people. **National Park Mountain** overlooks this famous campsite.

The Explorer's Museum at Madison Junction features exhibits about the Washburn Expedition and other early explorations and explains how Yellowstone became the world's first national park.

Madison Junction to Old Faithful

Facilities at Madison Junction include: ranger station, Explorer's Museum, amphitheater, campground.

Just beyond the bridge, a two-mile, one-way (south) road follows an old Indian trail through **Firehole Canyon**. Firehole Canyon Road passes between the 800-foot black lava walls of Firehole Canyon. From there you can see **Firehole Falls**, which drop 40 feet. Just below the falls, there's a swimming hole. You can take a refreshing dip!

Steam rises from hot springs along the Firehole River. (Photo by Mike Meloy)

Later on the white, churning water of the **Firehole Cascades** tears past banks of green grass and many-colored wildflowers.

The **Firehole River** is probably the river that mountain man Jim Bridger supposedly said ran so fast it got hot on the bottom. As it runs through the Upper, Midway and Lower geyser basins, the river is actually warmed by hot springs near its banks and below the surface of the water. You have to admit, though, the steam rising from the river would make a mountain man wonder what in tarnation was going on!

Somehow brown and rainbow trout and whitefish, which in most other places live in 67 degrees Fahrenheit, here have learned to live with the naturally high water temperatures of the Firehole. In some places along the river, the water temperature reaches 86 degrees Fahrenheit. Unnaturally hot water harms fish. Hot water from power plants and industries can cause diseases, throw off the fishes' life cycles and cause all sorts of problems. Apparently when the hot water is part of the natural environment, fish and other living things are able to adjust — naturally.

Water from Firehole Falls tumbles 40 feet. You can see the falls from Firehole Canyon Drive. (Photo by Dale Burk)

The Firehole River is another blue-ribbon trout stream. Ask again about fishing regulations.

Look around at the trees. Most of them are lodgepole pines. You know they are pines because all pines have clusters of two or more needles; lodgepole pines have two in a cluster. Lodgepoles grow so straight Indians once used them to built their lodges and tepees. That's how they got their name. You will see them everywhere in Yellowstone. In fact, they cover three-fourths of the park!

Run-off water from a hot spring meets the cold water of the Firehole River in Midway Geyser Basin. (Photo by Robin Tawney)

On the Grand Loop again, you'll travel for several miles up the Firehole Canyon. You'll come to **Nez Perce Creek** where it empties into the Firehole River from the east. The creek gets its name from the Nez Perce Indians who passed near here in 1877 on their way to Canada. They had been forced to leave their homeland in eastern Oregon and western Idaho. When they were told to move to a reservation, part of the tribe refused and escaped to find a new home. They were chased by the U.S. Cavalry. The Nez Perce fled through the park, and took some tourists hostage at this point. Several days later they released their hostages near the **Mud Volcano**, just north of Yellowstone Lake.

Imagine how afraid the hostages were and how desperate the Nez Perce must have been to find a new home where they could provide for their families. The Nez Perce were captured by the army just before they could cross into Canada and freedom, closing a sad, sad chapter in the history of the American West.

As you think about earlier times, watch for bison. They often graze in the meadows along Nez Perce Creek. Please watch them from a distance. Each year park visitors are seriously hurt because they forget that the calm-looking beasts are wild and they get too close. During the summer of 1983, 13 people were injured by bison, and one was killed.

Near here is **Fountain Flats Drive**, an old freight road that runs behind Lower and Midway geyser basins. In summer cars can travel three miles along this road until it deadends. From there the road continues as a bicycle and foot trail and rejoins the Grand Loop south of **Midway Geyser Basin**. In winter this old freight road is a one-way snowmobile and ski trail. You might want to hike or ski to **Imperial Geyser** and **Fairy Falls**. That is the only way they can be reached.

Can you tell what kind of force laid down the low, rounded hills to the left of the road? The shape and substance of these hills tell us that this area was once covered by a glacier. The hills are actually mounds of rock and rubble that were carried along by the glacier and laid down as it melted.

If you stay on the Grand Loop, just south of the turn-off to the Fountain Flats Drive, you'll come to the **Fountain Paint Pots**. In just a half-mile walk, you can see **Silex Spring**, **Morning Geyser**, **Fountain Geyser**, **Jet Geyser**, **Spasm Geyser**, **Jelly Geyser**, **Clepsydra Geyser**, the bubbling **Fountain Paint Pots** and — far out in the basin — **Kaliedoscope Geyser**.

This is the beginning of **Lower Geyser Basin**, the largest geyser basin in Yellowstone Park. Many groups of hot springs, most containing geysers, are scattered over nearly half the valley here. Chances are at least some of them will be erupting during your visit. This is a very active place!

As you walk along the boardwalk, notice how underground water helps create the geothermal features. Near the foot of the hill, where there is lots of water, you will see Silex Spring, a geyser with a pool so full it overflows a broad area. On up the hill, water is less plentiful. There you will find the Fountain Paint Pots. While the mudpots themselves might be larger elsewhere in Yellowstone, this is

the largest group of mud pots in the park. It has been growing since the 1959 earthquake shook things up. At one time
the pots threatened to swallow up the walkway. Only
fumaroles, or steam vents, are active at the top of the hill,
where water really is in short supply.

The white-socked trees you see are lodgepole pines that
were drowned when run-off water from the hot springs
changed its course. The bases of these trees have been turned to stone, or petrified, by minerals that have replaced the
wood. Trees with white socks are common in all the geyser
basins. Some have been standing this way for more than
100 years.

Great Fountain Geyser is one of the most spectacular geysers in the
world. Its eruptions last anywhere from 35 to 60 minutes. (Photo by
Robin Tawney)

Back on the Grand Loop, you will soon come to **Firehole
Lake Drive**. This three-mile, one-way road leads first to
Great Fountain Geyser, one of the most magnificent
geysers in the world. It erupts every 8 hours with many
powerful bursts, which sometimes reach nearly 200 feet.
Eruptions last anywhere from 35 to 60 minutes.

The Three Senses Nature Trail at Firehole Lake will help you appreciate things you might otherwise overlook. (Photo by Robin Tawney)

The Cook-Folsom-Peterson party of explorers discovered Great Fountain Geyser when they entered the Lower Geyser Basin for the first time in 1869. These men had come a long way to see if all the tall tales and rumors they'd heard were true. Just as they arrived in the basin, Great Fountain began to erupt. Imagine their excitement!

A member of the party, Charles W. Cook, later wrote, "We could not contain our enthusiasm; with one accord we all took off our hats and yelled with all our might."

If you come to the park in the winter, you probably will see a large herd of bison in the Lower Basin. Bison, elk and other animals move into the geyser basins to get away from deep snow because snow doesn't stay long here on the heated ground. They graze on plants that are able to grow in the basins year-round. The bison are particularly well suited because their thick, heavy fur insulates them from both heat and cold. They stay here until May when they move off to higher country, away from summer visitors.

The **Three Senses Nature Trail** is a special walk you won't want to miss. This is a rope-guided walk at **Firehole Lake** (which is really more of a pond) where you are asked to shut your eyes and use only your senses of smell, sound and touch. Blind visitors can read information provided by Braille labels along the trail.

Excelsior Geyser no longer erupts. It blew up its plumbing nearly 100 years ago. (Photo by Dale Burk)

Leaving Firehole Lake Drive, you are back on the Grand Loop where it crosses a low wooded rise to **Midway Geyser Basin** where a bridge across the Firehole River takes you to the major features. This geyser basin is small, almost totally confined to a narrow strip of land along a one-mile stretch of the river. Only seven geysers of any size can be found here, yet the Midway Basin is the site of the largest hot springs in the world — **Grand Prismatic Spring**. It is more than 370 feet across. And **Excelsior Geyser's** crater measures 200 by 300 feet. It is a wonder all by itself.

The ranger station at Old Faithful in 1917 was a peaceful place compared to the more modern version today. (National Park Service Photo)

Excelsior Geyser (which hasn't erupted since 1888) spills
out 5.8 million gallons of boiling water a day, enough to fill
more than 200 railroad tank cars or over 300,000
automobile gas tanks. When it was active, Excelsior blew
100 and sometimes 300 feet in the air. The explosive eruptions in its last 10 years tore its crater and its plumbing apart.
Excelsior is now actually leaking!

Hop back into your vehicle and ride two miles along the
wooded banks of the Firehole River on the Grand Loop
Road and you are at **Old Faithful** and the **Upper Geyser
Basin**. Watch for elk in the meadows as you drive.

**Facilities at Old Faithful include: ranger station,
visitor center, post office, lodging, restaurant, cafeteria,
snack shop, general store, photo shop, service station,
laundromat, public showers.**

Your first stop should be the information desk at the
visitor center. Ask the ranger naturalist what special programs are scheduled for the Old Faithful area. There are

almost always guided walks, self-guided trails, all-day hikes and evening programs. Get a schedule of geyser eruptions while you're there so you'll know what to watch for and when to watch. Geyser predictions change each day.

Old Faithful has been the symbol of Yellowstone National Park since the park was established in 1872. Without a doubt, it is the world's best-known geyser. Yet Old Faithful is not the largest, nor the highest nor the most regular geyser in Yellowstone.

Still Old Faithful is a good name for this geyser. Unlike most of the thermal features in Yellowstone, Old Faithful has changed very little in the last 100 years. Its heights, intervals and lengths of play are about the same as they were in 1870 when it was discovered and named by the Washburn-Langford-Doane Expedition. Those explorers thought Old Faithful looked like a "teakettle blowing its top."

Old Faithful has been the symbol of Yellowstone National Park for more than 100 years. Its eruptions are just about what they were in 1870 when it was discovered. (Photo by Robin Tawney)

Castle Geyser has the largest cone and may be the oldest of all the geysers in the park. (Photo by Robin Tawney)

The Upper Basin has more than 140 geysers, more geysers than anywhere else in the world. In fact the Upper Basin has more than one-fourth the world's total, all in less than one square mile. And most of the hot springs lie within a few hundred feet of the Firehole River.

Early Yellowstone visitors thought the Upper Geyser Basin looked a lot like a manufacturing center from far off. In fact, one 1903 visitor, John Burroughs, a naturalist and popular wildlife writer, commented during a trip to the park with President Theodore Roosevelt:

"Boiling lakes and steaming rivers are not common, but the new features seemed, somehow, out of place, and as if nature had made a mistake. One disliked to see so much good steam and hot water going to waste, whole towns might be warmed by them, and big wheels made to go round. I wondered that they had not piped them into the big hotels which they opened for us, and which were warmed by wood fires."

(Luckily for Yellowstone's geothermal features, the U.S. Congress decided to preserve them when it established

Yellowstone National Park in 1872. Tapping the steam would interfere with the geysers' natural action and would probably destroy them. That has happened to other geysers elsewhere in the world.)

Many of the geysers and hot springs were named during the early 1870s. The explorers of that time were awestruck by the wonders of the Upper Basin. While they thought all of Yellowstone was worth preserving, it was probably the Upper Basin that really convinced them.

Here you will see **Castle Geyser**, which looks like an old broken-down castle, **Grand Geyser**, which erupts to heights of 200 feet, and **Morning Glory Pool**, which has the shape and color of the morning glory flower.

You are in for a thrill when Grand Geyser erupts. It shoots bursts of water up to 200 feet in the air. (Photo by Robin Tawney)

Grotto Geyser got its weird shape when geyserite covered the trunks of trees that once grew right here. (Photo by Robin Tawney)

Try to spend as much time as you can in the Upper Geyser Basin. There is so much to see, it is impossible to take it all in on a short visit. Besides, it takes two or three days to wait for all the large and famous geysers to erupt!

"How can I spend days here?" you may ask. At first any geyser basin looks pretty barren, and may be boring if no geysers are erupting. But look closely and you'll see many plants and animals that have adjusted their lives to fit into the environment here.

Since the temperatures of the hot springs and geysers never vary, these plants and animals thrive year-round. Look for color in and around the springs and pools. Pale yellow or white ribbons of bacteria wave in the flow of the boiling springs. Yellow, orange, brown and green algae — tiny, tiny plants — grow in cooler waters.

See the flies above the orange and brown algae? They are getting their dinner. Other flies will eat their eggs and larvae. Dragon flies, spiders and birds will swoop in to eat both kinds of flies. This is really a lively community. You just have to be a good observer to see some of the forms of life.

If you visit the geyser basins in late winter, you'll see many wildflowers blooming — months earlier than in other parts of the park. That is because the ground is so much warmer here. The heat melts the snow as fast as it falls so that at least one plant blooms year-round. That plant — spurge — hugs the hot ground like a rug, growing in a tropical environment even when the temperatures may be zero degrees Fahrenheit just a few feet away.

If you visit in summer, you will see evidence of the basins winter residents. Look for elk and bison hoofprints that were mashed into the wet ground and scraps of manure.

Old Faithful to West Thumb

A short way along the road to West Thumb, you come to **Kepler Cascades**. A wooden platform offers you a wonderful view of this series of falls and cascades in the Firehole River, tumbling over 100 feet between steep canyon walls. Because it is upstream from the geyser basins, the Firehole here is unaffected by geothermal activity. Brook trout abound. This is another great place to fish.

Watch for water ouzels or dippers, the short and stubby dark gray birds that dive for insects at the bottom of fast-moving streams. Sometimes you may even see these clowns walking underwater.

Near the Kepler Cascades is a 2 1/2-mile foot and bicycle trail to **Lone Star Geyser**. Since the trail is really an old road, it is mostly paved and a great place to ride your bike.

Lone Star Geyser impressed trapper Osborne Russell in 1839 because of its peculiar cone, one of the largest in Yellowstone. The cone is 12 feet tall and very steep-sided.

Lone Star is a very regular geyser. It jets water 45 feet high for 30 minutes every three hours. If you happen to see Lone Star erupt, write the time and date on a slip of paper and put it on the sign marking the area. Your news will be much appreciated by those who follow you.

An all-day 7 1/2-mile hike from Lone Star Geyser will lead you over the Continental Divide to a very special place, **Shoshone Geyser Basin**, on the edge of **Shoshone Lake**. This is one of the few places in the park where you can see a major geyser basin in a totally natural state. No boardwalks, no cars, no crowds of tourists. You can easily pretend you are an explorer living in the 1800s. Back then Shoshone Basin wasn't anymore remote than other areas in Yellowstone.

Tiny Isa Lake is something else! The water that drains this pretty pond goes both east and west. (Photo by Robin Tawney)

The Shoshone Geyser Basin is one of the most important thermal areas in the world, despite its small size. About 40 geysers are found here within a 1,600- by 800-foot area. Most of the features were named by scientific survey teams in 1872 and 1878, when the last detailed studies and maps were made. Since the development of the park, Shoshone Basin has been "off the beaten path" and visited only by backpackers, horseback riders or canoeists.

If you do visit, be careful. Remember the crust around the geysers and hot springs is very thin and fragile. And don't throw anything — no matter how small — into the thermal features. Any object can clog the vents and maybe even stop eruptions.

Continuing east on the Grand Loop Road, you come to a tiny pond right on the Continental Divide at **Craig Pass**, 8,261 feet. This is **Isa Lake** and it is quite unusual. Its water flows both to the Atlantic Ocean and to the Pacific, but not like you'd expect. Water draining from the western edge of the pond — which you'd expect to go to the Pacific Ocean

— flows west to the Firehole River, then to the Madison, and finally east to the Missouri, Mississippi, Gulf of Mexico and Atlantic Ocean. Water draining the eastern edge of the pond — which you'd expect to go the Atlantic Ocean — flows east through several creeks and lakes to the Lewis River, then west via the Snake and Columbia rivers to the Pacific Ocean. Crazy? That's Isa Lake!

In a few miles the Grand Loop once again crosses the Continental Divide. This time the elevation is 7,784 feet. From here you have a glimpse of **Yellowstone Lake** for the first time. Then you will enter a long tunnel of dark green. A thick forest of lodgepole pines lines both sides of the road. This is a natural forest, kept that way by national park policy. No thinning is done here. Dead and fallen trees will eventually break down and become a part of the soil, enriching it for future growth.

Shoshone Lake is off the beaten track and well worth the hike. (Photo by Mike Meloy)

South Entrance to West Thumb

If you enter the park at the South Entrance, you'll start out next to the **Snake River**, a clear, smoothly flowing mountain stream with sandy banks. The river flows south here, on its way to Grand Teton National Park and then north through Idaho.

From the South Entrance, the road almost immediately begins to climb 2,000 feet up the edge of **Pitchstone Plateau**. The plateau was formed by lava ash that flowed from one of Yellowstone's most recent volcanic eruptions about 60,000 years ago. Pitchstone Plateau is just south of the Yellowstone Caldera. The lava ash is called Pitchstone and is a kind of rhyolite that is found in rock and soil all over the park.

As the road crosses the **Lewis River** bridge, you will have a good view of the 29-foot **Lewis River Falls**. The river, falls and **Lewis Lake** were named for Captain Meriwether Lewis of the Lewis and Clark Expedition. A little farther on, the highway runs next to Lewis Lake. Lewis Lake is the third largest lake in the park. Ask a ranger for a fishing permit and a copy of park fishing regulations and try your luck with the brown trout.

Facilities at Lewis Lake include: ranger station, amphitheater, campground, boat ramp.

After a six-mile journey through a thick pine forest, you will reach Grant Village.

Facilities at Grant Village include: ranger station, visitor center, amphitheater, campground, post office, lodging, restaurant, general store, service station, auto towing and repairs, boat ramp, laundromat, public showers.

You will learn about the wilderness value of Yellowstone National Park through exhibits in the Grant Village Visitor Center. A slide program is presented every half hour in the auditorium.

A short drive brings you to **West Thumb** and the Grand Loop Road.

West Thumb to Lake Junction

Facilities at West Thumb include: general store, service station.

If you s-t-r-e-t-c-h your imagination, you can see how West Thumb got its name. Look at the map. If you think **Yellowstone Lake** looks a bit like a hand, you can see why early explorers named this bay West Thumb.

As you look at the map, notice how the Thumb is almost perfectly round. That is because West Thumb is actually the crater of a volcano — a newer and smaller one inside the huge Yellowstone Caldera. At a maximum depth of 320 feet, the water here is deeper than any other part of the lake, which lies partly inside the big caldera. The average depth of Yellowstone Lake is 139 feet.

West Thumb is actually the same size as **Crater Lake**, another caldera, in Oregon. But since Crater Lake stands all by itself, it has its own national park!

Tom Collins Point is a natural rock jetty that bears the name of a man who visited it a long time ago. This is a good place to sit and think about what Yellowstone was like 100 years ago when few people came here. (Photo by Robin Tawney)

Feeling the cold water here, it may be hard to believe West Thumb is a hot spot, but it is. Just about two yards beneath the lake bottom, the mud is boiling hot! And since the magma from the volcano that created West Thumb is so close to the lake bottom, it creates some startling features.

Lakeshore Geyser is actually submerged in the lake for much of the year. Then it doesn't erupt. But when the low water of late summer leaves its cone "high and dry," Lakeshore will erupt every 35 minutes for about 10 minutes, spouting its hot water 25 feet high.

While they are often surrounded by water, the cone and hot pool of **Fishing Cone** poke out of the bay no matter what the water level. Fishing Cone rarely erupts, but when it does, it will spout water about two feet in the air for hours at a time.

The narrow (600-foot) band called the **West Thumb Geyser Basin** contains other interesting thermal features. **Abyss Pool** is filled with hot, clear water that reflects the brilliant blue of the sky. The **West Thumb Paint Pots** are colorful like the **Fountain Paint Pots** in **Lower Geyser Basin**, but are much less active.

From West Thumb, the Grand Loop takes you 23 miles along the west shore of Yellowstone Lake to Lake Junction. Looking out across the lake as you travel will give some idea of how big this lake really is. Yellowstone Lake is the largest mountain lake in the United States. It is about 20 miles long and 14 miles wide. Its shoreline is more than 100 miles long, although roads trace less than half that distance.

The snowy peaks you see across the lake belong to the **Absarokas**, the same mountains you pass through if you enter the park at Silver Gate, at the park's northeast corner. Absaroka (say Ab-sor-kuh) is the Indian name for the Crow Nation. The Crows roamed through this country and, for a while, the northernmost part of the park was part of the Crow Reservation.

As you travel along, watch for white pelicans gliding on the air currents above the lake. They ride the warm air so easily, they only have to flap their 9-foot wings once in awhile. These birds wade in shallow water and scoop up fish

The West Thumb Geyser Basin sits in and along the shore of Yellowstone Lake. (Photo by Robin Tawney)

with their big bills and store their catches in the pouches below their bills. Pelicans nest and breed on Molly Island in the southeast arm of Yellowstone Lake. Boats are not allowed to land there.

You'll see plenty of gulls here, too. Most are California gulls, an inland bird that makes its home here. If you see an adult gull up close, look carefully for a red mark underneath its bill. Baby gulls peck this spot to tell their parents they are hungry.

Some of the fish these birds are after are native cutthroat trout. Yellowstone Lake and River are home to the largest population of native cutthroat trout in the world. These fish got their name from the bright red or orange slashes across their throats.

Near Storm Point, search for a sandy, steam-heated bison wallow. Then dig like crazy to find the fumarole! (Photo by Robin Tawney)

If watching the pelicans, gulls, and other water birds fish makes you want to try it, you can stop at any number of the picnic areas and fishing access sites along the lake. The best way to fish Yellowstone Lake is from a boat, trolling very slowly and casting a variety of spinners like the Mepps and rooster tails. However you decide to fish, first find out about the fishing regulations for this lake and get a permit, then wet your line.

Next the Grand Loop reaches Bridge Bay and soon after that, Lake Village.

Facilities at Bridge Bay include: amphitheater, campground, marina, boat ramp. Facilities at Lake include: ranger station, medical service, post office, lodging, restaurant, general store, service station.

Ask a ranger for directions to **Storm Point** and **Tom Collins Point**. Both can be reached along the same lakeside trail. Storm Point is a rocky piece of land that juts out into Yellowstone Lake. You can see how it gets buffeted by storms. Just beyond the point, look for sand pits back from

Visitors used to line both sides of Fishing Bridge as they fished for spawning trout. People can no longer fish here so the bears can fish in peace. (Photo by Dale Burk)

the lake's edge. These are bison wallows, where the huge animals rest and roll during the winter. One is shaped like a funnel. With your hands, dig as fast and deep as you can at the lowest point. Suddenly you'll find hot sand! So that's why the bison like this spot in the winter. They have their own private steam-heated bed!

Further along the lakeshore, you'll find Tom Collins Point, a fairly flat jetty of rock. Tom Collins scratched his name into one of the rocks on this point. No one knows who he was, but he left his mark here a long, long time ago.

The **East Entrance Road** joins the Grand Loop in a few more miles. The river you see is the **Yellowstone**. All the water in Yellowstone Lake drains into this river. Downstream, as smaller rivers empty into it, the Yellowstone River becomes broad and slower moving. There are no dams along the Yellowstone as it moves north, west and then east where it meets the Missouri River in North Dakota. That makes the Yellowstone River the longest free-flowing river in the lower 48 states.

Crossing the river near the junction with the East Entrance is **Fishing Bridge**.

Facilities at Fishing Bridge include: visitor center, museum, amphitheater, RV sites, general store, photo shop, service station, laundromat, public showers.

The development complex at Fishing Bridge is a problem for bears. No one considered the bears and other wildlife when this area was developed in the 1920s and added to in the 1950s. Grizzly and black bears come to the Yellowstone River and other smaller streams near here to catch fish that are spawning, or laying their eggs. **Pelican Valley**, the area from Fishing Bridge and east of **Pelican Creek** is one of the best places for bears to live in all of Yellowstone. Its wide variety of habitats and food sources supports a variety of other kinds of wildlife, too.

The waters provide the bears with lots of food. Besides dining on fish, the bears nibble on berries, ants, mushrooms and carrion, or dead animals. And sometimes on the garbage or groceries that a camper in the trailer village doesn't store properly. With both bears and people sharing the same campground, sometimes people get hurt.

The National Park Service may eventually close Fishing Bridge to camping. It is a plan that has been under consideration for a long time. When you think about it, they have no choice. Yellowstone is a refuge where wild animals can live out their lives in a natural way.

East Entrance to Lake Junction

The East Entrance, like the Northeast Entrance, cuts through the **Absaroka Mountain Range**. You enter the park and climb quickly up, up to **Sylvan Pass** at 8,530 feet. Just over the top you will come to **Eleanor Lake** and then **Sylvan Lake**. You might want to stop at Sylvan Lake and cast your line. Here it is catch and release fishing only. (Don't forget your fishing permit!)

Beyond the lakes, the entrance road leads you down the mountains to **Yellowstone Lake**. For a great view of the lake, take the one-mile side road north to the **Lake Butte** overlook. This butte, or flat-topped hill, offers one of the

The sharp peaks of the Absaroka Mountain Range welcome visitors who enter the park at both the East and Northeast Entrances. (Photo by Mike Meloy)

best views of the huge lake. On a clear day, you can see the **Washburn Range** to the northwest, the **Central Plateau** directly across the lake to the west, and **Two Oceans Plateau**, where streams flow to both the Atlantic and Pacific Oceans, to the south. Way to the southwest, you should be able to see the Grand Teton Mountains some 60 miles away.

Back on the East Entrance Road, you will pass the steam vents and hot springs of **Steamboat Springs** right along the lakeshore. Watch for osprey, gulls, pelicans, ducks and trumpeter swans.

Then you are at **Mary Bay**, where steam from underground once exploded and left this neat little bay. Another "steam explosion" formed **Indian Pond**, a round little lake between Mary Bay and the entrance road. You might want to explore this quiet spot on your own or by joining a naturalist walk (ask at the Fishing Bridge visitor center).

The East Entrance Road passes Pelican Creek and joins the Grand Loop.

Lake Junction to Canyon Junction

From Fishing Bridge at Lake Junction, you follow the Yellowstone River north through the Yellowstone Caldera.

Right away you will see the apparently innocent **LeHardy Rapids**. They may seem like any other stretch of white water, but don't let looks deceive you: LeHardy Rapids tears over an area that is actually bulging — inch by inch — each year. The bulge here means the magma within the earth is rising. Could this be a new volcano? Scientists all over the world are watching this hot spot!

On beyond the rapids is another touch of mystery. A trail 2/3 mile long leads you through the **Mud Volcano** area. You will think you have entered another world. Witches and their monstrous brews come to mind. Caldrons of hissing and spitting mud bubble furiously. Even the trees in this bleak and barren landscape have been hard-boiled by the steam from the hot springs. And the smell! Hydrogen sulfide gas, the same gas that forms inside rotting eggs, will take your breath away! (That gas comes from the highly acidic water, which breaks down the volcanic rock and forms the mud pots.)

When they discovered it in 1870, the Washburn-Langford-Doane exploring party thought the Mud Volcano was one of Yellowstone's most remarkable features. Then the "volcano" was 30 feet across and exploded with a sound "resembling discharges of gun-boat mortar." Steam rose 300 feet (more than twice as high as Old Faithful) and mud spattered nearby trees some 200 feet up on their trunks!

When another exploring party visited Yellowstone the following year, the Mud Volcano wasn't nearly so spectacular. Its plumbing must have collapsed. Since then the Mud Volcano and the surrounding area have been constantly changing. The last major change occurred in the summer and fall of 1978 when a series of small, shallow earthquakes centered here. Heat increased and water began to flow. Old features grew wilder and new ones burst from the ground. This heated frenzy reached its peak a year later. The results are what you see now.

Does the Dragon's Mouth Caldron remind you of bubbling witch's brew? (Photo by Dale Burk)

The hillside used to be covered with green grass and trees. Not so today. It was seared and shaken by the earthquakes. Now it is called **Cooking Hillside**. Cooking Hillside doesn't have enough water to become a hot spring, yet the bare and steaming ground is almost too hot to touch. Temperatures near boiling have been recorded right on the bare ground.

The names of other features reflect their nasty nature: **Sizzling Basin**, **Churning Caldron**, **Black Dragon's Caldron**, **Sour Lake**, **Grizzly Fumarole** and **Dragon's Mouth**. Imagine what it was like for the Washburn party to see this place for the first time!

Just across the Grand Loop Road is **Sulphur Caldron**, the most acid spring found in Yellowstone. Its water has been compared to the acid inside a car battery. Sulphur Caldron is so potent it is eating away part of the parking area. See the steam rising? Its yellow color comes from all the sulfur (rotten eggs again!) in the spring.

Hayden Valley is an ideal place to watch for wildlife. Note the game trail in the left corner of this photograph. (Photo by Dale Burk)

This thermal area is on the southern edge of a broad, fairly flat valley, named after Dr. Ferdinand Hayden, who in 1871 explored Yellowstone for the U.S. Geological Survey. Hayden's Survey brought back scientific information as well as photographs and paintings that helped convince Congress that Yellowstone was indeed a special place and should be preserved.

Long ago, a glacier dammed **Hayden Valley** and filled it with water. When the water receded, the valley was left with a thick layer of sand. Since sand doesn't hold water very well, the valley floor now dries out quickly. Only hearty grasses and sagebrush can grow in the valley flats. But in these open meadows, watch for elk and deer and coyotes hunting for unsuspecting rodents and other small animals. You might see bison, too, although most will be with their herds in the mountains. You might even see a grizzly bear.

Mallards spend their summers along the Yellowstone River as it flows through Hayden Valley. You can easily spot the males with their bright green heads. (Photo by Jack Tuholske)

The Yellowstone River crosses Hayden Valley and forms small ponds and marshes where tall grasses and reeds grow. You could see moose along here. Keep a sharp eye out for migratory waterfowl, too. This valley is a natural sanctuary.

Also look for trumpeter swans, the big white birds that nearly became extinct. Great blue herons wade in the shallows on their long stilt-like legs, searching for fish, toads and insects. You might see their nests high in the tops of dead trees near the marshy areas. Canada geese look regal with their black heads and necks with white chin straps and grayish brown bodies. Watch for mallard ducks, feeding in the shallow water, heads down and tails up. Other ducks, Barrow's goldeneye and mergansers, dive into the river for fish. Ospreys dive feet-first into the water and usually come up with a fish. Pelicans wade and gulls float to scoop up their catches.

Away from the river, our national bird, the bald eagle, nests in the pines. (This bird is not really bald, it just has a white head.) You may also see marsh hawks, gliding a few feet above the grasslands and marshes as they look for rodents.

Twenty years ago the only "wildlife" you could see in Hayden Valley were fishermen. The banks were lined with them because this stretch of the Yellowstone River was (and is) one of the finest fishing holes in the park. The real wildlife had moved away. Finally in 1965 fishing was banned in Hayden Valley. After a while, the moose and waterfowl and other animals returned. Now the valley is the best place in the park to see wildlife.

The placid water of the Yellowstone River turns into a mad torrent as it rushes down the Grand Canyon of the Yellowstone. (Photo by Mike Meloy)

The Upper Falls of the Yellowstone River crash 109 feet to the canyon floor. Chittenden Bridge is in the background. (Photo by Robin Tawney)

At the northern edge of Hayden Valley, the Grand Loop crosses **Alum Creek**. It is said that mountain man Jim Bridger used to tell stories about how the creek's warm, mineralized waters would shrink a horse's hooves. Just one taste of the water will tell you where he got that idea: Alum Creek water will make you pucker up!

Just beyond the creek, the valley narrows and suddenly you see it — the **Grand Canyon of the Yellowstone**. Cross the Chittenden Bridge, park and follow the trail to view the **Upper Falls**, where the Yellowstone River tumbles 109 feet to the canyon floor. It is hard to believe that this is the same river that wandered so peacefully through the Hayden Valley! Here it is wild and violent, forever cutting away more rock and soil from the canyon.

As you look at the falls, you might start wondering how so deep a canyon was gouged out of the hard rock. One answer is that some of the rock is hard, but some of it is soft and easily whittled away. But the "why" of the canyon takes a little more explaining:

Downstream from Upper Falls is another waterfall with nearly three times the drop. This is Lower Falls. (Photo by Dale Burk)

Two million years ago, the Yellowstone River ran the other way. It began cutting a shallow canyon into the volcanic rock. Then ash from volcanic explosions 600,000 years ago filled this canyon, and the river recarved its channel, about where it is today, but still flowing in the opposite direction. A large lake formed just inside the north rim of the caldera. Eventually the lake rose and spilled northward into the head of the old canyon, reversing the flow of the river so that it ran the same way it does today. As the lake finally emptied, the river began to erode the thick lava flows upstream toward the present site of **Lower Falls**. Then about 300,000 years ago the new canyon area was covered by a glacier. The deposits left as the glacier melted filled up the canyon again. Two other glaciers covered the area and as they melted, the canyon was carved by the melting ice.

The canyon eroded quickly in places where the rock was soft. Other places, like the brinks (or tops) of the waterfalls, were hard and did not erode easily.

The canyon today looks about like it did 10,000 years ago, when the last glaciers melted. It is approximately 800 to 1,200 feet deep and 1,500 to 4,000 feet wide, and 20 miles long.

From the Upper Falls parking lot, you can take **Uncle Tom's Trail**, which was named for Tom Richardson, the man who built the first trail into the canyon in 1890. It was part of a special experience Richardson offered early Yellowstone tourists. After picking them at the hotel, which was then across the canyon, he would ferry his customers across the river above the Lower Falls. They would walk along the rim and then down 528 steps where they would get sprayed by the falls, eat dinner, then walk back up and ferry across to their hotel. All this for 50 cents a person. Visitors around the turn of the century always wore their best clothes when touring, so imagine the men in their top hats and women in their long, full wool skirts hiking up and down that trail!

Stand at the very brink of the Lower Falls and feel the power of water in a hurry. (Photo by Robin Tawney)

Chittenden Bridge made Richardson's enterprise obsolete, but you can still walk 500 feet down the steep series of modern stairways and paved ramps. You will end up about half-way to the canyon floor at the base of Lower Falls. It is an awesome sight to watch the water crash down 308 feet, twice the height of famed Niagara Falls in New York. Notice how much cooler it is here. Can you feel the force of the water as it thunders into the pool below?

Back up at the top of the canyon, visit **Artist Point**. Can you tell how this overlook got its name? Look at the many colors in the canyon walls. Do they remind you of an artist's palette? The rock at the top of the canyon is nearly black, other rocks are gray, light pink or lavender. Still other layers have been stained shades of orange and yellow, the yellow stone for which the park and river are named. (That yellow rock lining the canyon walls is soft, hydrothermally altered rhyolite lava.) The colors appear entirely different on foggy or sunny days, at dawn or twilight. What colors do you see today?

Notice the rock that looks like lightweight concrete with bits of rock embedded in it. This is welded tuff, formed when melted rock burst from a long-ago volcano and stuck together and hardened as it landed and cooled.

Continue up the Grand Loop to Canyon Village and turn east at the intersection to the North Rim Drive. The road divides in about a mile. Follow the left fork to **Inspiration Point**, about a mile away. Along this road you will see a great example of how glaciers moved the countryside around long ago. Right in the middle of all the volcanic rock sits a huge granite boulder — 24 by 20 by 18 feet. This 500-ton "glacial erratic" was pushed or carried by a glacier and carried 20 miles from the mountains in the northeast corner of the park. See how lodgepole pines have grown up around the boulder? It has been here for a long, long time.

From the parking area at the end of the road, a trail leads to Inspiration Point with its view up the canyon to the Lower Falls and beyond. The river winds through the canyon about 900 feet below.

Other trails along North Rim Drive lead to spectacular

A glacier pushed or carried this boulder some 20 miles before melting and leaving the huge piece of granite where it now rests. (Photo by Dale Burk)

views. You can watch the water fall right over the brink of Lower Falls by walking a 3/8-mile switchback trail that descends 600 feet. There you can see and feel the power of water in a hurry.

From several viewpoints, you can see what look like brushpiles high up in the rocks. Those are osprey nests. Like eagles, osprey mate for life and return each year to the same nest.

Look closely for violet-green swallows darting in and out of their condominiums or apartments along the canyon walls. They are strong and elegant birds in flight as they catch flying insects for their meals in mid-air. You will see lots of swallows from **Lookout Point**.

Facilities at Canyon Village include: ranger station, visitor center, amphitheater, RV sites, post office, lodging, restaurant, cafeteria, general store, photo shop, service station, horse rental, laundromat, public showers.

Canyon Junction to Norris Junction

You are now on the middle bar of the figure-eight that makes the Grand Loop Road. It is a short stretch — just 12 miles from Canyon to Norris.

For the first few miles, you will pass through a forest of lodgepole pines. This forest, like all the others in Yellowstone, is left in its natural state. That is National Park Service policy. To keep Yellowstone as natural as possible, in 1972 the National Park Service began letting natural fires burn themselves out, as long as they didn't endanger people or developments within the park. Before that time, the park put out fires, thinking that would help preserve the park in a natural state. Instead, it allowed an unnatural amount of "fuel" to build up on the forest floor, which caused an unnatural number of fires that park workers had to scurry to put out. Now, since fires are allowed to burn, the forest floor is burned clean after a fire and little "fuel" accumulates. Even when lightning strikes, only a small spot — maybe just one tree — is affected. As the "new" forest gets older, windfallen trees and needles build up and the burn cycle starts again. The Park Service has found that by allowing natural forest fires to burn, fewer fires actually occur.

You will be lucky if you spy a black bear like this one nibbling on berries or ants as you drive through a lodgepole pine forest. (Photo by Ed Wolff)

Watch for black bears along this road. If you see one and decide to stop, stay in your vehicle with the windows closed. Black bears are wild and dangerous. They are not Gentle Bens.

Eight miles from Canyon, the road cuts through **Virginia Meadows**, a beautiful open place full of wildflowers in season — red Indian paintbrush, deep blue-fringed gentian, bright blue larkspur, yellow sunflowers and lupines of anywhere from lavender to dark purple. Why aren't there trees here? The water table, the level of water underground, is too close to the surface. It is too wet for trees. Instead there is lots of grass, just right for the elk you can see grazing here in the early morning and early evening.

The swift **Gibbon River** flows through Virginia Meadows on its way to **Virginia Cascade**. The Gibbon is one river that begins — in the mountains around **Grebe Lake** — and ends — at its confluence with the **Firehole River** — right inside the park. Here the Gibbon supports mostly brook trout. You might want to try your luck.

A one-way east loop road will take you to the Virginia Cascade where the Gibbon River tumbles and foams down slippery rock, landing some 60 feet below.

In a few more miles, the road joins the west side of the Grand Loop at Norris Junction.

Canyon Junction to Tower Junction

Here you will follow the Grand Canyon of the Yellowstone, but you won't be able to see much of it from the road. The Grand Loop climbs to **Dunraven Pass** at 8,859 feet. The blur of unending lodgepole pine gives way to spruce and fir as you get higher and higher. Why do you think the trees change? Does it have something to do with elevation?

To the east you will see **Mt. Washburn**, a 10,423-foot mountain named after Henry D. Washburn, who led an official exploring party into Yellowstone in 1870. Washburn was surveyor general of public lands for the Montana Territory. The information he and others gathered helped lead to the establishment of Yellowstone National Park two years later.

Can you see the big box on top of Mt. Washburn? It is really a fire lookout station. You can hike up to the lookout for a great view of the park. If you do, you will walk 3.6 miles one way, so plan to spend most of the day on your hike. Remember to take along a warm jacket, rain gear and drinking water.

On a clear day, you can see most of the park from the summit, the very top of Mt. Washburn — its mountain ranges, Yellowstone Lake, Yellowstone River and parts of the Grand Canyon of the Yellowstone. You can even see the Teton Mountains, 100 miles to the south in Grand Teton National Park.

Here you can also see the Yellowstone Caldera. Mt. Washburn is at its northern edge and Yellowstone Lake is just inside its southern edge. Try to blot out all the trees and picture how the caldera might have looked when it first formed. Steam puffs from geothermal features here and there remind us that deep beneath the ground, the magma is still hot.

Watch for bighorn sheep jumping up and down the steep face of the mountain. Mt. Washburn is their summer home.

From Dunraven Pass, the Grand Loop drops into broad fields of sagebrush. Groves of shimmering aspen appear wherever water collects.

Across the Grand Canyon to the east, you can see **Specimen Ridge**. This is where Jim Bridger claimed he saw petrified birds perched on petrified trees singing petrified songs in which every note turned to stone.

The trees (and nothing else) were turned to stone, or petrified, 40-50 million years ago when they were covered with the hot lava ash from volcanoes and mud flowing down their slopes. Since some of the trees are still standing, scientists think they must have been slowly buried by the ash and mud flows, which choked them without knocking them over. Others were buried very quickly just like the trees in the path of Mt. St. Helens lava flows. Hot water mixed with dissolved minerals from the ash seeped into the dead trunks and turned them to stone.

The climate millions of years ago must have been a lot like Georgia's because the petrified trees are kinds that grow in a hot and humid climate, which Yellowstone definitely is not! Scientists have found magnolias, walnuts, oaks, dogwoods, hickories and sequoias in the petrified forests — not at all like the Douglas fir forest that grows here today!

You can't see the petrified trees from the road. You can reach Specimen Ridge only by an all-day hike from Tower Junction or from Lamar Ranger Station. Ranger-led hikes start at Tower.

While you are deciding how — and when — you will hike to Specimen Ridge, you'll probably continue on down the road to **Tower Falls**. Suddenly, you're there!

Facilities at Tower Falls include: ranger station, amphitheater, campground, lodging, restaurant, general store, photo shop, service station, horse rental.

Early rangers take a break outside the old Tower Soldier Station. (National Park Service Photo)

A footpath near the photo shop leads to a platform overlooking Tower Falls, a 132-foot waterfall on Tower Creek. The name for this falls really fits, doesn't it? The rocks surrounding the falls look like towers. Tower Falls didn't come by its name easily, however. It was named by the Washburn-Langford-Doane Expedition after much debate.

At the outset, members of the expedition agreed not to name any of the features after themselves. When they came upon Tower Falls, John Trumbull suggested they name it Minaret Fall, an appropriate name since a minaret is a slender tower. Samuel T. Hauser, however, objected to Trumbull's choice because he claimed it violated their agreement. Hauser claimed Trumbull chose "minaret" because he had a sweetheart, Minnie Rhett. Even though Trumbull denied naming the falls after his sweetie, the party decided to change its name to Tower. Later Trumbull and some of the other members of the Washburn party began to think Hauser had a sweetheart named Miss Tower, but it was too late to change the name.

(Despite the agreement these men had made not to name any natural features after themselves, they named Mt. Washburn after their leader on the same day they named Tower Falls!)

Back on the Grand Loop, you will soon drive beneath **Overhanging Cliff**, a formation of lava and stream gravel cemented together. The cliff leans out about 40-50 feet and actually overhangs the road!

Just before Tower Junction, you come to the narrowest part of the Grand Canyon called **The Narrows**. The canyon is 500 feet deep here. Right inside the entrance to The Narrows you can see a thin stone column, **The Needle**. The softer rock on the edges of of this pile of volcanic rock has been washed away by wind and water.

Stop at **Calcite Springs** and take the short round-trip trail for another look at The Narrows.

You soon reach **Tower Junction**, where the Grand Loop Road is joined by the Northeast Entrance Road.

Northeast Entrance to Tower Junction

If you enter the park here on the Montana-Wyoming border, you will have passed through the two old mining towns of Cooke City and Silver Gate, Montana. The road from Cooke City to Mammoth Hot Springs is open all year, but the road east from Cooke City is only open from June 1 to Oct. 15, so don't plan to enter the park from the Northeast Entrance in the winter!

The mighty **Absaroka Mountains** reach for the sky as you begin your visit to the park. You pass between two of the park's very highest peaks. **Abiathar Peak** (10,928 feet) is on the east side of the road and **Baronette Peak** (10,404 feet) is on the west. The road follows **Soda Butte Creek** down the valley between these mountains.

Eleven miles from the Northeast Entrance, you see **Soda Butte**, an old hot springs terrace. When the hot springs here was active, it built up layer after layer of calcium carbonate, a kind of limestone. Just like in any hot springs, hot water dissolved the limestone and brought it out of the ground, where it was deposited and hardened once again. And like other hot springs, Soda Butte is colored by algae that live in its warm water.

The road now follows the **Lamar River** through the broad **Lamar Valley**. A great glacier flowed through this valley 10,000 or more years ago. You can tell there was a glacier here because glacial erratics, those huge granite boulders, are scattered everywhere. They were carried by the ice flowing down from the mountains to the north and then stranded as the ice melted. The glaciers also formed the shallow depressions and ponds you see here.

Watch for waterfowl in the Lamar River. You may see Barrow's goldeneye and mallard ducks. This is a good place to look for pronghorns, bison and elk, too. You can see them grazing in the open, grassy meadows.

Here you also can find the **Lamar Ranger Station**, where the Army once raised bison just like ranchers raise cattle.

When the Army first took over the park in 1886, Yellowstone was one of the last places in the United States to be a home to bison. At one time nearly 60 million bison roamed all over this country, but people shot them for their meat and to control the Indians by killing their source of food and clothing. White men also shot bison by the hundreds for sport and for their meat and hides. Bison pelts made warm robes and bison leather had many uses.

When the bison trade ended in 1884, the only wild bison remaining were those that lived in the mountains of Yellowstone Park. By 1898, the park superintendent estimated that only 50 of these mountain bison remained. The army began bringing in animals from herds in Montana and Texas, where ranchers raised domesticated bison. These animals were bred with the wild mountain bison. Today, long after that project ended, the park has about 2,000 animals.

This bull bison grazes away the spring months in the Lamar Valley. He is shedding his winter coat. (Photo by Ellen Knight)

The Slough Creek Valley is robed in winter white. This is a peaceful place anytime of the year. (Photo by Mike Meloy)

Lamar Ranger Station also is the home of the Yellowstone Institute, which offers a variety of seminars and camps to teach both adults and children more about Yellowstone National Park. Their programs for kids includes a three-day camp at the Buffalo Ranch. If you would like to learn more about their special programs, you can write to The Yellowstone Institute, Box 515, Yellowstone National Park, Wyoming 82190.

South of the Lamar Valley is **Specimen Ridge**. You can hike there from the Lamar Ranger Station. To get there from here, you will have to cross the Lamar River. The river can be dangerous at times, so be sure you get advice from a ranger before you set out. (See the section in this guide on the Northeast Entrance to Tower Junction for a description of Specimen Ridge.)

Near the ranger station is **Slough Creek**, a quiet place to spend the night off the beaten track. A two-mile trail from the campground drops into **Slough Creek Valley**, a place of aspens, open ponds and lots of animals — moose, mule deer, elk, ducks and coyotes. Watch for golden eagles soaring, picking up air currents off the rocky cliffs as they search for rodents. This trail is an old wagon road. Imagine yourself on a bumpy buckboard, touring the park in earlier times. Do you think you'd miss the comforts of home?

As you get closer to Tower Junction, notice the trees. The needles on the branches closest to the ground have been stripped of their needles by browsing elk and deer!

Tower Junction to Mammoth Hot Springs

Just after leaving Tower Juction, you can take a 1 1/2-mile side road that leads to a **Petrified Tree**, the only one in the park that is close to a road. This tree is really a stump, the remains of a redwood that grew here in a forest 40-50 million years ago. Like the petrified trees on Specimen Ridge, this tree was turned to stone after being covered with volcanic ash.

Several other tree stumps used to stand near this one, but early visitors carried them away. Remember: "Take only pictures, leave only footprints."

Back on the Grand Loop, you can see that the forest is beginning to open up again. You can see Rocky Mountain juniper now and sagebrush tells us this country is dry. Only about 18 inches of snow and rain fall here each year.

There are lots of small lakes and ponds in the open areas. Look closely and you can see where beavers have built their dams. The gnawed-off aspens and cottonwoods around the ponds are a giveaway. Watch for ducks, geese and swans.

North from **Elk Creek** on the Grand Loop Road, the grooved and wrinkled **Garnet Hill** comes into view. Its rocks are some of the oldest on earth. Scientists believe these granite rocks may be a billion years old! They contain imperfect gemstones, garnets. Look, but don't take any with you.

Up ahead, the terraces of Mammoth Hot Springs look like ancient ruins.

President Theodore Roosevelt spoke at ceremonies dedicating the Roosevelt Arch at Yellowstone's North Entrance in April, 1903. (National Park Service Photo)

North Entrance to Mammoth Hot Springs

As you enter the park from the edge of the little town of Gardiner, Montana, you will pass through the **Roosevelt Arch**, dedicated by President Theodore Roosevelt in 1903 when the Army ran the park. Roosevelt was a conservationist and Yellowstone Park was very special to him. He supported the park's goals and defended it against destruction and overdevelopment throughout his life.

Right away you can tell that this part of the park is warm and dry. Only 13 inches of rain and snow fall here each year. Because its climate is fairly mild, the North Entrance is the only park entrance that is really accessible to wheeled vehicles year-round. The Northeast Entrance is also open, but once you leave the park, you cannot travel any farther than Cooke City.

If you do enter the park in the winter through the North Entrance, you will see mule deer, pronghorns and bighorn sheep right along the road.

The low shrubs you see are sagebrush. This is pronghorn antelope country. Watch for them on your drive to **Mammoth Hot Springs**. And listen for meadowlarks calling to one another.

Not far from the North Entrance, you will come to the 45th parallel of latitude. Here, as measured on the earth's surface, you are exactly half-way between the equator and the north pole!

A ways farther, you will wind up a hill, past the grade school and homes of park employees, and you'll see the gray stone buildings of Yellowstone National Park Headquarters at Mammoth Hot Springs.

Mammoth Hot Springs to Norris Junction

Facilities at Mammoth Hot Springs include: superintendent's office, Horace M. Albright Visitor Center and museum, amphitheater, campground, medical service, dispensary, post office, lodging, restaurant, general store, photo shop, horse rental, service station, auto towing and repair.

The gray stone and tan frame buildings here were built when the Army was in charge of the park. They sit atop an old hot spring terrace that some early visitors, like Rudyard Kipling, author of "The Jungle Books," thought might cave in any minute. In a letter, Kipling noted: "The ground rings hollow as a kerosene-tin, and someday the Mammoth Hotel, guests and all, will sink into the caverns below and be turned into a stalactite."

What do you think?

Twice a week all summer long, a ranger-naturalist dresses up like a soldier of 1915 and gives walking tours of the old Fort Yellowstone. Ask about these tours at the visitor center. They really bring history to life.

The Horace M. Albright Visitor Center has a very nice museum of natural and park history and a movie about the park's early history and the origin of the national park idea. It also is the home of the Yellowstone Library.

The Mammoth Terraces are turning inside out through the work of nature's miner, water. About two tons of dissolved limestone are brought to the surface each day! (National Park Service Photo)

If you are lucky enough to visit Yellowstone in the winter, you will see elk strolling on the sidewalks of park head-quarters and browsing in the yards of park employees. Temporary fences are put up everywhere to protect shrubs.

Like the bison, elk also were once threatened by overhunting. Until 1883 when hunting in the park was outlawed, elk were slaughtered by the thousands for their hides and ivory teeth. (All elk have two ivory teeth that are prized for their value as jewelry. Some early members of the Elk's Club used the ivory teeth for stickpins and cufflinks.)

When the U.S. Army Cavalry began to administer the park in 1886, it cracked down on poachers, people who illegally killed elk, and began to treat Yellowstone as a wildlife refuge. In 1911, when the Army believed that the population of elk had become too big for natural predators, disease and weather to control, the Army began feeding the elk and protecting them from their animal enemies.

Between 1921 and 1929 elk were treated like farm animals, fed in the winter and protected from predators. Later elk were moved to other areas outside the park or killed by hunters when they migrated on their own to winter range outside the park to reduce numbers. At one time they were shot inside the park by park personnel. Today no trapping or hunting occurs in the park, and elk are once again the most numerous grazing animal in the park. About 16,000 animals are part of the northern herd. Their population now is controlled by the amount of food available, by the harsh winter weather, and by hunting outside the park in areas to which the elk might migrate.

Liberty Cap is the skeleton of an ancient hot spring. (Photo by Dale Burk)

Hot water flows everywhere at the top of this terrace at Mammoth Hot Springs. (Photo by Dale Burk)

As you drive past the hotel and restaurant complex on your way to the hot springs and terraces, you'll see a trail that takes off just beyond the last commercial building. The **Beaver Ponds Trail** is an easy six-mile loop walk where you may see ducks, elk, deer and sandhill cranes. In the spring, you may even see a bear after it awakens from its winter sleep. But don't get near: Bears are wild and potentially dangerous.

Back on the Grand Loop Road heading toward **Norris Geyser Basin**, you can't help but notice the **Liberty Cap**, an ancient natural cone 37 feet high and 20 feet around at its base. The Liberty Cap once was a hot spring. Hot water would flow from the opening at its top, depositing limestone and forming a cone. The cone finally got too high and choked off the water rising in the spring. The Liberty Cap was named in 1871 by a government exploring party because it looked a lot like the caps worn by colonial patriots during the Revolutionary War. Look for other odd and graying formations around the park. They will also be the "skeletons" of ancient hot springs and geysers.

Immediately after Liberty Cap, you will reach the very base of the Mammoth Hot Springs terraces. A self-guiding nature trail explains the hydrothermal activities to be seen from the boardwalks. Wherever you go in Yellowstone's geothermal areas, stay on the trails and boardwalks. The water is hot and the ground has a fragile crust that could give way, just as Rudyard Kipling said, to an underground thermal area.

If the wind is blowing in the right direction, you will immediately notice the smell of rotten eggs. The smell comes from hydrogen sulfide gas dissolved in the water and being released when the water comes out of the ground.

The Mammoth Hot Springs and terraces are constantly changing. It is easy to see why. About 500 gallons of hot water per minute flow out of the terraces. And the water brings two tons of dissolved limestone to the surface each day. That's about how much four average-size horses would weigh! You are watching nature's miner at work as hot water turns this hillside inside out.

The **Upper Terraces** can be reached by a one-way road that loops for 1 1/2 miles. Here water collects in a series of basin-like pools. When the top basin is filled, the water flows over the lip and drips down to other basins below.

Notice the gnarled and twisted trees on the Upper Terraces. Why do you think they look that way? These junipers may be the oldest living things in the park.

Driving now toward Norris Junction, you will pass through a cut in the mountains called **Golden Gate**. The name comes from the yellow lichens, a kind of tiny plant, that cling to the bare rock. Golden Gate was formed by volcanic eruptions 600,000 years ago.

You now come to **Swan Lake Flat**, a dry, open area covered with sagebrush. Although dry, Swan Lake Flat still gets more than 1 1/2 times as much rainfall as Gardiner at the park's north entrance. You sometimes see trumpeter swans around **Swan Lake** and the big open marshy areas. You may see moose here, too. Moose live along lakes, ponds, swampland and river bottoms where they can eat tender willow shoots and other shrubs that grow there.

A short spur road takes you to **Sheepeater Cliff**, where a band of Sheepeater Indians lived when they were the only people living year-round in Yellowstone. The cliff is made up of columns of basalt lava rocks that are gradually breaking up and tumbling down

Just beyond this cliff is **Obsidian Cliff**, Jim Bridger's famous mountain of glass. The Sheepeaters and other Indians who lived outside the park used the glassy obsidian

Watch for moose along Obsidian Creek as it parallels the road. (Photo by Mike Meloy)

rock to make arrowheads, knives and scrapers. It is hard to see why Bridger thought this cliff looked like it was made of glass because today moss and lichens have covered most of it. Look for patches of the shiny black obsidian here and there. The shiny rock was formed when molten lava cooled quickly, instead of slowly like the lava in much of the park. Maybe the lava flow hit a glacier. That would sure cool it fast!

Obsidian Cliff isn't as interesting as it used to be because park visitors took home pieces of obsidian for souvenirs. Protect your park by leaving the rock where you find it and urge other visitors to do the same.

You might see moose along **Obsidian Creek** as it parallels the road.

On down the road, you'll see a dead-looking hill to the east. **Roaring Mountain** is especially impressive in the early morning when you can see steam columns rising from its steaming and hissing vents. Early visitors named the mountain in 1902 when they heard a single steam vent roar. Then Roaring Mountain fell silent once again. Or did it? Can you hear any roaring today?

Porcelain Basin looks like a moonscape. There is hardly any plant life or color here. (Photo by Dale Burk)

Just before you reach Norris Junction, you will see **Old Norris Soldier Station**, an Army outpost from days gone by. There is a small campground nearby that is a good place for picnic or an overnight stop.

Norris Junction to Madison Junction

Facilities at Norris include: museum, ranger station, amphitheater, campground.

A short spur road from the junction leads to **Norris Geyser Basin**. Norris Geyser Basin was named for Philetus W. Norris, who served as Yellowstone's second superintendent from 1877 to 1882. Although he did not discover the basin, his explorations and reports were largely responsible for calling attention to this area.

Right away you can see that this geyser basin is different from others in the park. Although the geysers may look similar to others you've seen, the basin looks like a moonscape. There is almost no plant life and no color, especially in **Porcelain Basin**. The ground and formations are all a drab gray. Only the stream channels have a little color, and then only a bit of green from algae or chemical compounds.

Norris looks different because the water here isn't like the water found in the other basins. This water is highly acidic because a lot of sulfur is brought to the surface with the hot water. The acid makes the geyserite, the mineral that is deposited and forms the crust around the geysers, different, too. At Norris the geyserite is spiny, not beady like it is in the **Upper Basin** where it is deposited by alkaline water.

To get an idea of the difference, think of acid as lemon juice and alkali as milk. Although the acids and alkali in the water of geysers basins are not at all like lemon juice and milk, you can guess that they are very, very different.

Norris is hotter and more active than any other geyser basin in the park. In fact it is one of the hottest and most active basins in the world. The hot rock that provides the heat for the hot springs is probably less than a mile beneath your feet! The geysers and hot springs here are more restless than in other areas in the park. A new hot spring might come to life overnight. Sometimes it might last for months or years, or it might be gone again in a few days.

Norris is hotter and more active than any other geyser basin in the park. This colorless pool boils madly. (Photo by Dale Burk)

Something funny happens nearly every year at Norris in late summer. No matter what the weather has been like, all of a sudden practically every spring and geyser becomes muddy. Pools that are normally quiet spring to life and become powerful geysers. After a few days or a few weeks (remember, geysers aren't all that predictable), everything returns to normal and the water runs clear. No one is sure why this happens, but is probably related to the water table, the level of underground water.

Since the thermal features are constantly changing, the ground is unstable and can be very dangerous. Park rules say you must stay on the trails and boardwalks leading through every geyser basin. If you step off the paths, the thin crust could break and drop you into a steamy pocket of scalding hot water. These rules were made to protect you from serious burns and help preserve the features you see. Park rules also say no pets in the geyser basins. You wouldn't want your curious dog to wander into trouble.

Be sure to stop at the Norris museum and ask the ranger naturalist what's new in the geyser basin and when some of the more permanent geysers might erupt. You can tour the area with a naturalist or take a self-guided walk. The museum will help you understand what you are seeing.

Norris Geyser Basin is made up of two distinct areas called **Porcelain Basin** and **Back Basin**. Trails to each basin begin at the museum. Each trail is about a mile long.

Porcelain Basin is constantly changing. Even the biggest, longest-living geysers are never quite the same from one year to the next. Mini-geysers spring up all the time. Some are spouters — geysers that are small and short-lived. While they are active, they sput-sput water a few feet all the time. Each time they spout, they deposit minerals within themselves so they soon seal themselves in. The hot water they were throwing up has to find its way out, and it does through another new geyser. Look for spouters in the central part of the Porcelain Basin, especially on the flat area beyond **Pinwheel Geyser**. How many spouters can you find?

Many of the changes that occur in the geyser basins hap-

In contrast to Porcelain Basin, Back Basin is skirted by lodgepole pines, making it a pleasant place to see geothermal features on a hot day. (Photo by Dale Burk)

pen because of earthquakes that shake the ground. These tremors usually affect the underground plumbing systems of geysers and hot springs and that affects their activity. See if you can tell whether any of the thermal features has changed recently. When in doubt, ask a naturalist.

If you are at Norris on a hot summer day, you will enjoy a walk through the cool lodgepole forest of the Back Basin. There you will find two of Yellowstone's most famous geysers. **Steamboat Geyser** was once the most powerful geyser in the world. It got its name because the tall column of steam that puffs up every few minutes reminded early visitors of a steamboat. While Steamboat still throws up 40 or so feet of steam and water every day, its last major eruption was in September, 1984. Then it threw water nearly 400 feet into the air. Everything got soaked, including the cars in the parking lot! Its water phase lasted 20 minutes, followed by over 40 hours of bellowing steam. Steamboat is still unpredictable. It could erupt again anytime.

Echinus is one geyser you won't want to miss. Watch it go through its cycle of draining and refilling. (Photo by Robin Tawney)

You can really see how a geyser works when you stop by **Echinus Geyser**. The name comes from the spiny geyserite that surrounds the geyser pool. Early visitors thought the geyserite looked like sea urchins or tide-pool animals called echinus by the Greeks.

Watch the Echinus pool fill with water and begin to boil. Soon water shoots up in a great explosive bursts of steam and water that sometimes go over 75 feet in the air. The eruption usually lasts five minutes or so and occurs every 45 to 75 minutes. After the explosion, the pool drains and begins to refill. Listen for the gurgling as the vent drains after every eruption. Does the whole thing remind you of a toilet?

Back on the Grand Loop, on your way now to **Madison Junction**, you cross a grassy meadow called **Elk Park**. Watch for elk in Elk Park, especially early or late in the day.

The road follows the **Gibbon River**.

In the small canyon between Elk Park and **Gibbon Meadows**, you'll find the **Chocolate Pots**. These mud pots are stained a rich reddish-brown from iron oxide. Do they look like chocolate to you? The riverbed is iron-stained, too.

You next come to the grassy **Gibbon Meadows**. You will find a lot of interesting hot springs here.

You can reach the **Artist Paint Pots** by a forested half-mile trail at the south end of the meadows. These bright colored mud springs bubble merrily. Like other hot springs, they get their colors from minerals and hot water algae. While you admire these pots, watch for elk grazing in the meadows.

Watch for elk in Elk Park along the Gibbon River. (Photo by Dale Burk)

The Gibbon River meanders quietly and then tumbles 84 feet down
Gibbon Falls at the edge of a volcanic caldera. (Photo by Dale Burk)

Across the Gibbon River Bridge on the west bank is a
steep mile-long trail leading to **Monument Geyser Basin**.
You can see how this basin got its name. Geysers have built
up weird cones by their spraying eruptions. **Thermos Bottle
Geyser** is the only one that is still active. There is no other
place like this in the park.

Stop at **Gibbon Falls**, where the water tumbles 84 feet
over the eroded rim of a caldera. It is another reminder of
Yellowstone's wonders. Just before the water falls over the

brink, the Gibbon Rivers is only ankle deep — you could walk across. Then the water falls in thundering white sheets, and once again becomes a peaceful, grassy banked stream.

As you watch the falls, you may be pestered by golden-mantled ground squirrels and bright-eyed chipmunks. Please don't feed any of the park's wildlife. Junk-food junkies can't stay healthy for long in the wild. They become too dependent on human foods and may stop eating natural foods.

Just before you reach Madison Junction, stop to see **Terrace Spring** with its gorgeous algal colors. If you cross the road, you can take a trail to the top of **Purple Mountain**. There you can see where the Gibbon and Firehole rivers join to form the Madison River.

The Grand Loop is joined by the West Entrance Road at Madison Junction.

When you are in it, Yellowstone seems plenty big. So it may surprise you that the park is still not big enough to make sure its animals and geothermal features are protected. (National Park Service Photo

THE GREATER YELLOWSTONE

Now that you've gotten to know Yellowstone Park, this news may come as a surprise. The true Yellowstone is much larger than its borders.

That is because Yellowstone National Park is part of an ecosystem that includes several million more acres around its boundaries. What is an ecosystem? An ecosystem is a self-contained natural unit. All the plants and animals within that ecosystem get everything they need to live right there.

How do we know Yellowstone National Park isn't an ecosystem all by itself? For one thing, when the boundaries were drawn long ago, they were drawn without any real knowledge about what kind of space animals need or how activities outside the park borders might affect them or the hydrothermal features.

Now modern research tells us that some animals leave the safety of the park to feed at various times of the year. We know that the deer and elk of Yellowstone require specific kinds of food and cover to stay alive and healthy. Grizzly bears have even greater requirements. And the geologic faults that help form the many wonders of the park extend far beyond the park's borders.

It is not anyone's fault that the boundaries were drawn like they were and that they don't include all the land the animals need to survive or the hydrothermal features need for their protection. The research just wasn't available. Let's be glad that the boundaries were drawn when they were to protect at least a major portion of the area.

But now that we know where the Yellowstone ecosystem is, we need to do something to protect those areas outside the park so we can continue to protect the resources of Yellowstone Park itself. How do we do that? First, we need to learn more about the Greater Yellowstone Ecosystem.

Greater Yellowstone Ecosystem

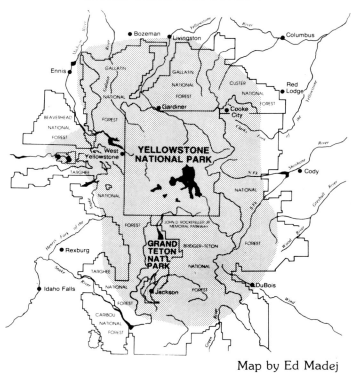

Map by Ed Madej

The Greater Yellowstone Ecosystem

The Greater Yellowstone Ecosystem includes Yellowstone and Grand Teton national parks, two national wildlife refuges, six national forests, portions of three states — Montana, Wyoming and Idaho — and 13 counties. Each one of those parks, refuges, forests, states and counties writes its own rules and has its own plan for managing resources, even though all are a part of the Greater Yellowstone Ecosystem.

Remember, in nature, everything affects everything else. That is why pressures in each portion of the Yellowstone ecosystem threaten the whole area. For example, all around the boundaries of Yellowstone Park, logging, mining, recreational development, and oil and gas drilling threaten the park's grizzly bears, elk and bison.

Yellowstone's grizzlies are threatened by developments outside the park boundaries. (Photo by Montana's Department of Fish, Wildlife and Parks)

These developments disturb the animals because they mean that lots of people and heavy machinery will make a big fuss, build roads and clear the land. All this will make the animals look for a new place to live.

The animals of Yellowstone don't realize when they are stepping across the borders of the park. They don't know when their habitat — their homes and ranges — is not protected. That is why management of the whole ecosystem is so important.

Many of Yellowstone's bison and elk, for example, leave the park each winter to find food at a lower elevation where the weather is less severe. Sometimes their paths are blocked by roads, fences, homes or small towns. Sometimes they move into a rancher's pasture near the park and eat his winter hay supply.

When bison wander out of the park, the results can be deadly. Park bison may carry brucellosis, a disease that causes pregnant domestic cattle to lose their calves. Even though bison are not affected by brucellosis, domestic cattle are, so, unless the bison can be herded back inside the park, the shaggy beasts are shot. During February, 1985, nearly 90 bison were killed when they wandered out of bounds. Right after that, the Montana legislature passed a new law that allows bison to be hunted as big game animals.

Elk that winter outside the park may be shot, too. Montana has a late season elk hunt just outside the park boundaries where many elk spend the snowy months. Each year hundreds of elk are legally killed. Sometimes bull elk are illegally shot inside and outside the park by people who sell their antlers to be ground up and used for medicinal purposes. Antlers sell for hundreds of dollars — even more when they are still growing and are covered with a soft velvet-like skin. Sometimes the elk are drugged and left alive, though their antlers are sawed off.

Since thousands of bull elk shed their antlers each spring in the park, many poachers steal what they find on the ground. (Remember, it is illegal to take anything from Yellowstone.) The U.S. Fish and Wildlife Service estimates that 28 tons of elk antlers are illegally collected each year in Yellowstone and turned into a $30 million business!

Threatened Grizzly Bears

Poachers also kill grizzly bears inside and outside the park. The bears' claws, heads, hides and gall bladders are worth a lot of money on the black market. Other bears are killed when they have run-ins with man.

Grizzly bears are listed as threatened by the federal Endangered Species Act. That means they will be in danger of dying out if they and their habitat are not protected. Grizzlies are particularly endangered because the females may not breed until they are 5-8 years old. Then the females care for their one or two cubs for two to three years, and produce no more cubs during that time. You can see that if too many grizzlies are killed, the bears may disappear altogether.

Grizzlies outside the park also may be killed by hunters. The state of Montana allows 25 bears to be killed each year. That number includes those bears that are killed illegally as well as those that are legally hunted. The hunting season

CLOSED

AREA BEHIND THIS SIGN IS
CLOSED TO HUMAN TRAVEL
DANGEROUS BEAR

Sometimes the Park Service closes trails to give the bears more room to roam. (Photo by Dale Burk)

automatically stops when the 25-bear limit is reached. Since grizzlies need many, many acres of wilderness to live undisturbed, they include the entire ecosystem as their home. Some of the bears that are killed could be Yellowstone bears.

Pressures inside the park affect the animals, too. For the grizzly, that means as more and more people come to the park each year (more than 2 million do now), the Park Service has to think up ways to protect both the bears and the visitors.

During certain times of the year, some parts of the park are off-limits to humans so the bears can feed in peace. In other parts of the park, such closures may become more permanent.

For example, the National Park Service plans to eventually close the Fishing Bridge development at the northern end of Yellowstone Lake. The Fishing Bridge area is part of the best grizzly bear habitat in the park. As grizzlies wander from the Yellowstone River to Yellowstone Lake seeking natural foods, some inevitably find garbage or improperly stored groceries in the development. Because bears remember where they get a good meal, one that has gotten human foods usually returns to the feeding site and becomes a "problem" bear. That bear is trapped and taken to a more remote area. If it returns again and again, it may be killed.

The Fishing Bridge development was supposed to be closed when the new tourist complex was built at Grant Village. According to plans, the Grant Village development would replace the one at Fishing Bridge. While Grant Village is also grizzly territory, it is not as critical as the Fishing Bridge area. Loud and organized opposition — from recreational vehicle groups and other special interests — has temporarily delayed the closure. Now both Fishing Bridge and Grant Village welcome visitors and the bears are left with less room to roam.

Yellowstone's fragile geothermal features are protected, but they could be affected by activities outside park boundaries. (Photo by Robin Tawney)

Geothermal Pressures

The animals of Yellowstone are not the only resources to feel pressure. While the hot springs and geysers of

Yellowstone are protected inside the park, they could still be drastically affected by activities that take place outside the boundaries.

Just 13 miles west of Old Faithful, some people would like to tap the hot water formations within the Island Park Caldera. No one knows whether those geothermal features are connected through their complex plumbing to those in Yellowstone Park and whether, if the features outside the park are drilled, the drilling and extraction of geothermal heat would shut down Old Faithful and other geysers. Even if Old Faithful didn't stop spouting, the drilling could permanently change the features of Yellowstone. No one can really know that unless drilling takes place. Then it could be too late.

What we do know is that Congress established Yellowstone National Park in 1872 to totally protect its thermal features. And that tapping underground hot water sources has destroyed seven out of 10 of the world's major geyser basins in the last 30 years.

How You Can Help

If it sounds like Yellowstone needs help, it does. But what can you do? You can visit the park and its surrounding area and learn more about the plants and animals and how they relate to each other by reading, observing and spending time with naturalists. A few days at the Yellowstone Institute or the Teton Science School will help you learn even more. For a list of classes offered by each school, write the Yellowstone Institute, Box 515, Yellowstone National Park, Wyo., 82190, or the Teton Science School, Box 68, Kelley, Wyo. 83011.

For more information, write the Yellowstone Library and Museum Association, Box 117, Yellowstone National Park, Wyo. 82190. YLMA publishes books, pamphlets and maps on Yellowstone Park and sponsors the Yellowstone Institute.

Follow articles about the Yellowstone area in your local newspaper and national magazines. Join the Greater

Yellowstone Coalition, an organization of groups and individuals trying to make sure the ecosystem is preserved. The Coalition will keep you informed and help you take action. Write the Greater Yellowstone Coalition, Box 1874, Bozeman, Mont. 58715.

Write your congressional representatives and ask them to support legislation that requires management of the Greater Yellowstone Ecosystem. Tell them why you think it is important.

The future of Yellowstone National Park depends on wise decisions. Do your part to help your park. We all need to speak for those who cannot speak for themselves — the grizzlies, the elk, the bison, the hydrothermal features of the Greater Yellowstone Ecosystem.

Remember your Yellowstone lesson: Everything affects everything else. Use what you've learned about Yellowstone to make a difference.

YELLOWSTONE JOURNAL

This is the place to write about the things you see while you are in Yellowstone Park. Maybe some of the features have changed since this book was printed. Make a note, draw a picture. Writing about what you see will help you remember.

BIBLIOGRAPHY

Listed below are other books and articles that will help you get to know Yellowstone National Park. Read and enjoy.

Bartlett, Richard A. **Nature's Yellowstone**. Albuquerque: University of New Mexico Press, 1974.

Bryan, T. Scott. **The Geysers of Yellowstone**. Colorado Springs: Colorado Associated University Press, 1979.

Burk, Dale. **Montana Fishing**. Stevensville, Mont.: Stoneydale Press, 1983.

Christiansen, Dr. Robert L. **Statement Before the Subcommittee on Public Lands and Reserved Water**. Committee on Energy and Natural Resources, U.S. Senate, Casper, Wyo., Dec. 12, 1981.

Cundall, Alan W., and Lystrup, Herbert T. **Hamilton's Guide to Yellowstone National Park**. West Yellowstone, MT.: Hamilton Stores, Inc., 1981.

Dasmann, Raymond F. **Environmental Conservation**. New York: John Wiley & Sons, Inc., 1968.

Haines, Aubrey L. **Yellowstone National Park: Its Exploration and Establishment**. Washington, D.C.: U.S. Department of the Interior National Park Service, 1974.

Hampton, H. Duane. **How the U.S. Cavalry Saved Our National Parks**. Bloomington: Indiana University Press, 1971.

Keefer, William R. **The Geologic Story of Yellowstone National Park**. U.S. Geologic Survey Bulletin 1347, reprinted by the Yellowstone Library and Museum Association, 1976.

Kirk, Ruth. **Yellowstone: The First National Park**. New York: Atheneum Press, 1974.

Langford, Nathaniel Pitt. **The Discovery of Yellowstone Park**. Lincoln: University of Nebraska Press, 1905.

Martin, Christopher. **Your National Parks: Yellowstone**. New York: G.P. Putnam & Sons, 1965.

National Parkways: **A Photographic and Comprehensive Guide to Yellowstone National Park**. Casper, Wyo.: National Parks Division of World-Wide Research & Publishing Co., 1976.

Sax, Joseph L. **Mountains Without Handrails**. Ann Arbor: University of Michigan Press, 1980.

Schullery, Paul. **Old Yellowstone Days**. Boulder: Associated University Press, 1979.

Smith, Robert B., and Christiansen, Robert L. "Yellowstone Park as a Window on the Earth's Interior." **Scientific American**, February, 1980, Vol. 242, No. 2.

Yellowstone Staff. "The Integration of Visitor Use and Preservation of Aquatic Ecosystems in Yellowstone Park." **The Naturalist**, Summer, 1979, pp. 31-35.

INDEX

N

O

Y